D1554544

"The basic difference between an ordinary person and a warrior is that a warrior takes everything as a challenge while an ordinary person takes everything as a blessing or a curse."

Carlos Castaneda

Dedicated to the business warriors throughout the world

SCIENCEOFSTRATEGY.COM
Books, Seminars, and Training in Strategy

Mastering Strategy Series
THE GOLDEN KEY TO STRATEGY: EVERYDAY STRATEGY FOR EVERYONE
SUN TZU'S THE ART OF WAR PLUS THE ANCIENT CHINESE REVEALED
SUN TZU'S THE ART OF WAR PLUS ITS AMAZING SECRETS
THE WARRIOR CLASS: 306 LESSONS IN STRATEGY

Current Events Series
SUN TZU'S THE ART OF WAR PLUS STRATEGY AGAINST TERROR

Business and Career Series
NINE FORMULAS FOR BUSINESS SUCCESS: THE SCIENCE OF STRATEGY
MAKING MONEY BY SPEAKING: STRATEGY FOR MARKETING EXPERTISE
SUN TZU'S THE ART OF WAR PLUS THE ART OF SALES
SUN TZU'S THE ART OF WAR PLUS THE ART OF MANAGEMENT
SUN TZU'S THE ART OF WAR PLUS STRATEGY FOR SALES MANAGERS
SUN TZU'S THE ART OF WAR FOR THE BUSINESS WARRIOR
SUN TZU'S THE ART OF WAR FOR WARRIOR MARKETING
SUN TZU'S THE ART OF WAR PLUS THE ART OF CAREER BUILDING

Life Strategies Series
SUN TZU'S THE ART OF WAR PLUS THE WARRIOR'S APPRENTICE
THE ANCIENT BING-FA: MARTIAL ARTS STRATEGY
SUN TZU'S THE ART OF WAR PLUS THE ART OF PARENTING TEENS

Audio and Video
SUN TZU'S THE ART OF WAR AUDIO: NARRATED BY GARY GAGLIARDI
SUN TZU'S THE ART OF WAR PLUS THE ART OF SALES AUDIO
SUN TZU'S AMAZING SECRETS SEMINAR AUDIO: 2-CD SET
SUN TZU'S AMAZING SECRETS SEMINAR VIDEO DVD

Sun Tzu's

THE
ART
OF
WAR

FOR THE

Business Warrior

Strategy for Entrepreneurs

Sun Tzu's
THE
ART
OF
WAR
FOR THE

Business Warrior
Strategy for Entrepreneurs

by Gary Gagliardi

Clearbridge Publishing

Published by
Clearbridge Publishing

FIRST EDITION
Copyright 1999, 2000, 2001, 2006 Gary Gagliardi

Clearbridge Publishing and its logo, a transparent bridge, are the trademarks of
Clearbridge Publishing.

Manufactured in the United States of America.
Interior and cover graphic design by Dana and Jeff Wincapaw.
Original Chinese calligraphy by Tsai Yung, Green Dragon Arts, www.greendragonarts.com.

Publisher's Cataloging-in-Publication Data
Sun-tzu, 6th cent. B.C.
 [Sun-tzu ping fa, English]
 Business warrior: strategy for entrepreneurs / Sun Tzu and Gary Gagliardi.
 p. 192 cm. 23
 Includes introduction to basic competitive philosophy of Sun Tzu
 ISBN 978-929194-39-1; 1-929194-39-0
 1. New business enterprise—U.S. 2. Small business—U.S. 3. Home-based business. 4. Military art and science—Early works to 1800. I. Gagliardi, Gary 1951–. II. Business warrior.
HD62.5 2002
658.11 —dc21

        Library of Congress Catalog Card Number: 2006902145

Clearbridge Publishing's books may be purchased for business, for any promotional use,
or for special sales. Please contact:

The Science of Strategy Institute: Clearbridge Publishing
PO Box 33772, Seattle, WA 98133
Phone: (206)533-9357 Fax: (206)546-9756
www.scienceofstrategy.com
info@clearbridge.com

Contents

Business Warrior:
Strategy for Entrepreneurs

Note: The thirteen chapters of *Business Warrior* follow the original thirteen chapters of Sun Tzu's *The Art of War*. After a one-page introduction, each chapter has our award-winning translation of *The Art of War* on the left-hand pages and our adaptation for the business warrior on the facing right-hand pages. Chapter titles combine Sun Tzu's original chapter name with the topic on which we focus our application of his ideas.

Business as a War for Survival

To be successful as an entrepreneur, you need to understand that business is a continuous battle for survival. If you don't think like a business warrior, you will have a very short life as an entrepreneur. Eighty percent of small businesses go out of business within their first two years. Most successful entrepreneurs learn the rules of strategy from the painful and costly lessons of trial and error.

This book offers a simpler and more rewarding approach: learning how to apply the principles of strategy to business competition. It uses the world's most respected guide to strategy, Sun Tzu's *The Art of War*, as a template for explaining how you survive and prosper from the battles of the marketplace. In reading it, you will discover that most of your competitors do not understand what strategy is or how to use it. One of the reasons the rules of strategy work so well is that so few people know how to use them correctly.

How does *The Art of War* apply to successfully starting, running, and growing your own business? The Chinese title of this work, *Bing-fa*, means literally "competitive skills." Unlike other works on military strategy, Sun Tzu designed his book to explain the secrets of competition in the broadest terms possible. The only differences between competition in the marketplace and military warfare are the types of tools used and the nature of the battleground. The only weapon that this book teaches you to use is the most powerful competitive weapon of all—the human mind.

Sun Tzu's *Bing-fa* teaches you to use your unique position in the

競 (vertical Chinese characters in left margin)

孫
子
兵
法

competitive environment to discover opportunities while turning your opponents' apparent strengths against them. This is the
essence of being a successful entrepreneur. *The Art of War* offers a
powerful, nonintuitive system for decision-making. It solidifies
your vague idea of a strategy into a clear, well-defined set of rules.
Bing-fa teaches that only a few key factors influence the outcome of
your efforts. Success goes not to the strongest or most aggressive
but to those who best understand their situation and what their
alternatives really are. When you have mastered Sun Tzu's system,
you will be able to instantly analyze competitive situations, spot
opportunities, and make the best decisions for your business.

In our adaptation for the business warrior, the basics of *bing-fa*
are tailored to help you in the struggle to survive while competing
against much larger competitors. As in all our *Art of War* books,
we present our entrepreneurial interpretation side by side with
our complete award-winning translation of the original *Art of
War*. While *Business Warrior* applies Sun Tzu's ideas in ways that he
would never have foreseen, it does so respecting the integrity of the
entire system of strategy that reaches back almost 2,500 years. The
Science of Strategy Institute has spent literally decades perfecting
this material.

Sun Tzu's principles are simple and direct. The underlying
concepts that these principles are built on, however, are rich and
complex. This book is meant only to give you a feeling for how
those principles are used by entrepreneurs. One of our goals for
this book is to get you interested enough in these ideas to want to
master them, and the Institute offers the best such training in the
world.

People mistakenly see war and, more generally, competition as
an adversarial, destructive process, but Sun Tzu saw it as a necessary component of a productive world. Familiar with the poten-
tially destructive nature of war, he teaches you how to minimize

the costs of competition through good strategy. From good strategy, you learn how to discover new market possibilities, how to work with and sell to customers, and how to be successful with minimal risk.

In developing this special version for entrepreneurs, we are faithful in adapting the concepts of strategy from the military arena to the business world. We simply define the competitive marketplace as a battleground for sales and customers. The military generals addressed by Sun Tzu become today's business warriors. The nation for whom the army fights becomes the business that you are trying to help survive. The contested terrain translates into the particular marketplace that you serve.

What makes this interpretation so natural is Sun Tzu's economic view of competition. In the second chapter of *The Art of War*, GOING TO WAR, Sun Tzu reflects on the costly nature of war. The secret to competition, he concludes, is not just winning battles; it is winning in a way that enriches the nation. The secret is not victory alone; it is making victory profitable. The concept of balancing unpredictable costs against elusive rewards is the basis of all strategy.

This economic view of strategy maps extremely well onto any serious approach to building a business. Your goal in having your own business is not just winning sales, getting work to do, or outshining your competition; rather, it is making a profit in a way that grows your business over the long term. Any business can do well for a day or a year. The real challenge is leveraging each step forward so that your business has even greater opportunities in the future.

Though *The Art of War* shows you how to find success in competitive situations, Sun Tzu's recipe for success is to avoid unnecessary conflict. He sees such conflict as inherently costly. He teaches you how to handle direct, hostile confrontations when they cannot be avoided, but good strategy defuses these situations before they occur.

Strategy is largely an exercise in group psychology: you must convince customers, potential customers, employees, and competitors to give you what you want without a fight. You must convince potential opponents and rivals that it is not worth their time and effort to go after your customers. Sun Tzu taught the persuasion power of strategy as an alternative to destructive confrontations in competitive situations such as price wars.

In building your business, your first goal is to survive, but your larger purpose should to create a business that can survive easily, without you working twenty-four hours a day to make ends meet. As an entrepreneur, your only resource is your time. That time is limited. Good strategy teaches you how to use your limited time as effectively as possible to create a self-sustaining organization. The goal is to win business easily, at a profit, and with minimal risk.

The first step in building a self-sustaining business is understanding your strengths and weaknesses compared to those of your competitors. You only want to go after customers who you are likely to win. You also want to be certain that winning those customers is well worth the cost.

The lessons of strategy are extremely specific about what to do in certain situations. You must pay close attention to the details of your business situation. You must recognize different business stages, different types of opponents, different decision-making mistakes, different competitive signals, and so on. When adapted for business warriors, these detailed lists from the ancient rules of strategy are surprisingly complete.

Good strategy offers a "cooperative" view of competition. According the rules of strategy, you cannot win through your own efforts alone. You don't create your business opportunities. You can only leverage opportunities created by the weaknesses of your opponents. The secret is recognizing a good opportunity when it presents itself. Strategy teaches that it is easy to get so bogged down in relatively unrewarding business activities that you overlook the real keys to your eventual success. You must learn how to let the needs of customers shape your business if you want to have a successful career as a business creator.

Strategy is knowledge-intensive. The knowledge of how to perform a certain task is not enough. Victory goes to the business warrior who best understands his or her competitive position and how to advance that position. Creativity has a special and important place in this realm of competitive information. Business innovation and continual improvement flow naturally from applying the rules of strategy.

The universal utility of the principles of strategy means that you can apply them in different ways in different situations. For this reason, you should read and reread *Business Warrior* at least once a year even if you don't go on to study strategy in more depth. With every reading, you will develop more insight into how you can apply good strategy to your current situation. As your situation changes, different parts of the book will become more important.

This book introduces you to the science of strategy and how it applies to business competition. It will give you a sense of how strategy works and how you can use it to make better decisions. However, it is certainly not our most extensive explanation of the rules of strategy or even the principles in *The Art of War*. It is meant only as an easy and rewarding introduction to these powerful principles.

✦ ✦ ✦

The Elements of Strategy

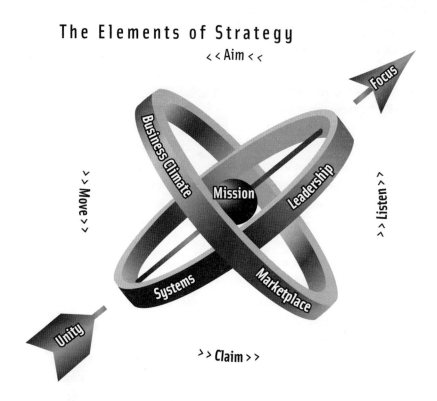

> > Move > >

Focus

> > Listen > >

Business Climate

Mission

Leadership

Systems

Marketplace

Unity

> > Claim > >

Sun Tzu first described the key elements of strategy 2,500 years ago in *The Art of War*. In our basic translation, these five elements are called "philosophy," "climate," "ground," the "commander," and "methods." In our business adaptation, we call them the *mission*, the *business climate*, the *marketplace*, *leadership*, and *systems*. Whatever terms we use, these five elements completely define a competitive position. All the other components of strategy—unity, strength, knowledge, battle, and so on—have very specific and logical relationships to these five elements of a strategic position. The depth and sophistication of this system is best understood if you spend a little time exploring these interrelationships before reading the text.

Sun Tzu teaches that every competitive situation depends upon the unique position of a competitor within the larger competitive environment. The core of any strategic position is what Sun Tzu called a philosophy but what we also call a business mission. The other four key elements define two integrated systems. The first is the competitive environment. It consists of the climate and the ground, or, in business terms, the business climate and the marketplace. The second is the competitor, a commander and methods, or, leadership and the systems that make a business work.

The focus on the competitive environment was a unique feature of Sun Tzu's work, at least until Darwin. As with so many of Sun Tzu's basic concepts, he describes the environment as two opposite and yet complementary halves. These halves are the climate (heaven) and ground (earth). Together they mark the time and place in which competition occurs.

Climate is the realm of time and change. Like the heavens, climate is beyond our direct control. The continuous change of the climate affects all other aspects of a strategic position. The fact that climate is always changing means that your strategic position is always changing as well. This means that no position is completely stable. If you don't do anything to respond to these changes, you will become their victim instead of their master. This is why strategy teaches that you must always look for ways to advance your position because changes in climate are always eroding it.

Ground is both where we fight and what we fight over. For a business warrior, the ground is the marketplace, the place in which the competitive battle for customers takes place. Unlike the business climate, which is largely beyond your control, the most important aspect of the marketplace is that you choose your place within it. Positioning, in a strategic sense, is the science of positioning yourself within the market. Choosing the right markets, moving to them, and utilizing them are the goals of your decision-making.

Within this competitive environment, each competitor has

unique characteristics that also define his or her position. We break these characteristics down into two critical components, the competitor's leadership skills and the competitor's systems. The basic purpose of all strategy is to provide decision-making methods for leaders.

A leader is the person who makes the key decisions. All entrepreneurs are, by definition, leaders. You must decide what needs to be done on the front lines of battle. Leadership is the realm of the individual and character. Successful organizations are not run by committees. They are run by strong individuals who can make good decisions. You must master the principles of strategy so that you can make the right decisions quickly.

Methods or business systems are the techniques of organization. Business systems are, by definition, the realm of group action and interaction. Even if you are the only person in your organization, all of your systems for doing business are built around working with others. In larger organizations, you need more complicated systems to work with greater numbers of people. The decisions of leaders shape the business systems of organizations.

This brings us back to the business mission or philosophy. Mission is the unique idea around which an organization is built. A clear, consistent philosophy provides a strategic position with *unity* and *focus*. The marketplace is infinite in its potential size. Climate swings between the extremes of change. Leaders come and go. Methods evolve. A core philosophy binds a competitive organization together and defines its relationship with the outside world. A mission is a shared goal that binds together an organization's employees, customers, and suppliers.

These five core elements are the framework for understanding all other strategic concepts and methods. You cannot apply any of the other principles of strategy unless you first understand your strategic position. Like a balance sheet, your strategic position provides you with a snapshot of a current condition. You must constantly compare your position with the positions of others. To use strategy, you must have a good understanding of your relative strengths and weaknesses compared to those of others. Without this checkpoint, you are unable to plot your strategic course forward. In other words, you are unable to make consistent progress.

The goal of strategy is to advance your strategic position over time. Without an understanding of your position, you cannot even define what an "advance" really is.

There are many "opportunities" for making money in the short term that can destroy your strategic position over the longer term. Opportunities must serve your mission to take you in the direction that you want to go. If opportunities run against the business climate, they are too short term. If opportunities take you away from your existing market, you will lose your current customer base. If opportunities are not suited to your individual character as a leader, they will not work out well over time. If they do not fit your existing systems, they will not end up being profitable.

Real opportunities build on your existing position rather than working against it. You can build a very different position over time, but you must use whatever strategic assets you have as the starting place for building that position.

The science of strategy teaches that four steps are absolutely necessary to advance your position over time. At the Science of Strategy Institute, we describe these steps as *listen*, *aim*, *move*, and *claim* because these terms are less ambiguous and more straightforward than the terms "knowing," "foreseeing," "moving," and "positioning" that Sun Tzu uses in the *The Art of War*.

Every type of advance in position can be broken down into these four components, but all the principles of strategy can also be classified as falling into one of these four skill areas. Each step defines entire categories of strategic knowledge. These four external skills are also defined in terms of the four external key elements.

The leadership skills are listening and aiming. Listening gathers information about the competitive ground, that is, the marketplace. Aiming makes decisions targeting an opening created by the changes in the climate. Listening requires intelligence. Aiming requires courage.

The method or business system skills are moving and claiming. Moving acts to take advantage of a new opportunity. Claiming uses your new position to reap a reward. Moving requires speed. Claiming must be consistent with your mission.

All four skills or steps are required to make any progress in advancing your position. No matter how much work you put into the other steps, you still need all four together. Otherwise, it is like building a bridge missing one of its spans. It doesn't matter how well you complete the other spans—no traffic is getting over until all four are completed. People who listen but cannot make decisions are just an audience. People who aim without moving are just dreamers. People who move without claiming are just dancers.

These four skills create an endless cycle. Listening leads to aiming. Aiming necessitates moving. Moving requires claiming. Claiming triggers more listening.

The leadership skills, listening and aiming, are intellectual skills, turning information into decisions. The systems skills, moving and claiming, are action skills, turning decisions into concrete changes. The cycle is an economic one; listening and moving are costs, and aiming and claiming are their rewards.

In *The Art of War,* these four skills are frequently referenced through metaphors. Listening is symbolized as sound. Thunder, music, and drums are all metaphors for listening and the knowledge that it brings. Aiming is described as vision. Colors, lightning, and so on are all metaphors for aiming. Moving is "foot work," which in the military means marching. Marching is a concrete form of changing positions. Claiming is variously described as gathering food, building, eating, digging, and so on.

The five elements defining a strategic position are described in the first section of the first chapter. The balance of the work describes the many different aspects of using the four skills of listening, aiming, moving, and claiming. For example, the first chapter, **ANALYSIS**, and the last, **USING SPIES**, explain the key techniques for listening. Other chapters may focus primarily on one of the skills or describe the many important relationships between them.

Sun Tzu organizes his work very much like a work of classical mathematics. He starts with the most basic principles, the five key elements, and then builds on those principles throughout the work. In the original Chinese, the work read much more like mathematical equations. Any English translation is by necessity a simplification of these original Chinese formulas.

In reading this work, you will get a strong sense for how strategy works and some great ideas about how you can apply strategy to the business challenges that you face every day. At the Science of Strategy Institute, we offer a wealth of other books and products to help you understand both Sun Tzu's text and the science of strategy in more depth. *Business Warrior* is just a great place for any entrepreneur to start mastering these techniques.

This chapter began with a diagram of the five elements that define a strategic position and the four skills that advance a position. Such diagrams were used in classical Chinese science and medicine to show the conceptual relationships among the key components of a system. This diagram now also serves as the logo for the Science of Strategy Institute.

Chapter 1

Analysis: Understanding Strategic Positions

Many people think that strategic analysis is the same as business planning, but in most respects, strategic analysis is the opposite of traditional planning. Strategic analysis is about understanding. Planning is about control.

Planning works in stable, controlled environments. Strategy is what you need for dynamic, competitive environments. In a controlled environment, your plan determines what happens. In a competitive environment, conflicting plans come together to create something that no one planned. Planning deals with internal organizational needs. Strategy focuses on external environmental needs.

Strategy begins with competitive analysis. Strategic analysis begins with the five key factors that define a strategic position. The factors are used to compare your competitive situation with that of your competitors. You need more complete information for competitive analysis. This means questioning what you think you know and going outside your normal circles to gather information.

In strategic analysis, you never take information for granted. You need to control what your opponents know about you and you need to suspect what you hear about others. In classical strategy, communication is the realm of deception, where more people are either self-deluded or mislead by others. In the end, all strategic analysis is a matter of carefully balancing conflicting information and the pros and cons to arrive at the best possible decisions to move forward.

Analysis

SUN TZU SAID:

This is war. 1
It is the most important skill in the nation.
It is the basis of life and death.
It is the philosophy of survival or destruction.
You must know it well.

[6]Your skill comes from five factors.
Study these factors when you plan war.
You must insist on knowing your situation.

1.	Discuss philosophy.
2.	Discuss the climate.
3.	Discuss the ground.
4.	Discuss leadership.
5.	Discuss military methods.

[14]Start with your military philosophy.
Command your people in a way that gives them a
higher shared purpose.
You can lead them to death.
You can lead them to life.
They must never fear danger or dishonesty.

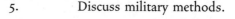

STRATEGY:

Strategy is the skill of advancing positions. Analyze your position by looking at five simple factors.

Understanding Strategic Positions

THE BUSINESS WARRIOR HEARS:

1 This is competition.
The ability to compete is the critical business skill.
Your decisions determine business survival or failure.
Your decisions lead to prosperity or poverty.
You must know what you are doing.

Five factors decide your business's success.
Evaluate these factors when analyzing the competition.
You must know your real position exactly.

1.   Analyze your business mission.
2.   Analyze the business trends.
3.   Analyze your target market.
4.   Analyze your decision-making skills.
5.   Analyze your business systems.

Strategic analysis begins with your mission.
You must define your business so that it shares a
higher purpose with others.
Your business can hurt other people.
Your business can improve people's lives.
People must feel safe doing business with you.

MISSION:

*Mission is the
core of your
position. A clear
mission creates
strength and
focus in your
new venture.*

POSITION:

Your position exists within a larger competitive environment, which you do not control.

[19]Next, you have the climate.
It can be sunny or overcast.
It can be hot or cold.
It includes the timing of the seasons.

[23]Next is the terrain.
It can be distant or near.
It can be difficult or easy.
It can be open or narrow.
It also determines your life or death.

[28]Next is the commander.
The leader must be intelligent, trustworthy, caring, brave, and strict.

[30]Finally, you have your military methods.
They include the shape of your organization.
This comes from your management philosophy.
You must master their use.

[34]All five of these factors are critical.
As a commander, you must pay attention to them.
Understanding them brings victory.
Ignoring them means defeat.

DECISION:

Good strategic decisions are based on analyzing how these five factors together create your position.

Next are the economic trends.
The business climate can change from good to bad.
Your product can go from popular to unpopular.
These economic trends will change continually.

Next is your target market.
You can target distant customers or local ones.
You can choose difficult customers or easy ones.
You can target customers who are large or small.
Your target market determines your success or failure.

Next are your leadership skills.
You must be a learner, an accountant, an enthusiast, a salesperson, and a manager.

Finally, you need to define your business systems.
You must organize the work so that it creates value.
Your procedures depend upon your mission.
You must master effectiveness and efficiency.

All five factors are important.
You must pay attention to them all.
Your choices here determine your success.
You will fail if you take any of them for granted.

> **AIM:**
>
> *Your ability to foresee and leverage changes in the environment is the key to your marketing success.*

> **LEVERAGE:**
>
> *Your unique business opportunities come from your unique position within the larger environment.*

You must learn through analysis. 2
You must question the situation.

3You must ask:
Which government has the right philosophy?
Which commander has the skill?
Which season and place has the advantage?
Which method of command works?
Which group of forces has the strength?
Which officers and men have the training?
Which rewards and punishments make sense?
This tells when you will win and when you will lose.
Some commanders perform this analysis.
If you use these commanders, you will win.
Keep them.
Some commanders ignore this analysis.
If you use these commanders, you will lose.
Get rid of them.

Plan an advantage by listening. 3
Adjust to your situation.
Get assistance from the outside.
Influence events.
Then analysis can find opportunities and give you control.

RELATIVITY:

No position is good or bad in itself. You only understand positions by comparing them to others.

2 You need to study and analyze each business factor. You must constantly question your assumptions.

You must ask:
What is the real purpose of my business?
Do I have the needed decision-making skills?
When and where can I create additional value?
How should my business be organized?
How is my business going to beat the competition?
Why does my business do the work more effectively?
Do my pricing and products make sense?
This analysis tells whether or not a business can succeed.
You must ask these questions over and over again.
If you strengthen your plan, you will be successful.
Keep at it.
Most people don't perform this careful analysis.
They think they will succeed just by working hard.
This is why 80 percent of new businesses fail.

3 Analysis forces you to listen to other people.
The more you know, the stronger your business will be.
Get help from those who know your industry.
Know the reality of the situation.
Analysis uncovers opportunities, focusing your energies.

MYOPIA:

If you fail to get an outside perspective on your position, you will miss most business opportunities.

Warfare is one thing. 4
It is a philosophy of deception.

³When you are ready, you try to appear incapacitated.
When active, you pretend inactivity.
When you are close to the enemy, you appear distant.
When far away, you pretend you are near.

⁷If the enemy has a strong position, entice him away from it.
If the enemy is confused, be decisive.
If the enemy is solid, prepare against him.
If the enemy is strong, avoid him.
If the enemy is angry, frustrate him.
If the enemy is weaker, make him arrogant.
If the enemy is relaxed, make him work.
If the enemy is united, break him apart.
Attack him when he is unprepared.
Leave when he least expects it.

¹⁷You will find a place where you can win.
You cannot first signal your intentions.

CONTROL:

Strategy is based on using the power of information. You control others by controlling their perceptions.

4 Competition comes down to one thing.
You must know who is fooling whom.

If you are new, you must appear experienced.
If business is slow, you must appear busy.
If you are anxious, you must appear calm.
If you are worried, you must appear enthusiastic.

If competitors have a good idea, take it as your own.
When customers are uncertain, help them decide.
When competitors are good, you must be better.
When competitors are strong, find a different business.
If customer decisions are emotional, play to emotion.
If competitors are weak, make them overconfident.
If competitors win easy sales, make them work for them.
If competitors have partners, steal the partners away.
Go after competitors who don't expect competition.
Avoid competing in ways that competitors expect.

You will find an opportunity that assures profit.
You cannot give others the idea of copying you.

TESTING:

You can mislead others and they can mislead you. Successful entrepreneurs continually test information.

Manage to avoid battle until your organization can 5
count on certain victory.
You must calculate many advantages.
Before you go to battle, your organization's analysis can indi-
cate that you may not win.
You can count few advantages.
Many advantages add up to victory.
Few advantages add up to defeat.
How can you know your advantages without analyzing them?
We can see where we are by means of our observations.
We can foresee our victory or defeat by planning.

PATIENCE:

*Consciously
choosing not
to act is just as
important as
acting decisively
when the time is
right.*

5 Before starting a new enterprise, you must know that you can make a profit.

You can only make a profit if you add a lot of value to a product.

Before you get into market competition, your analysis may show that you cannot win enough customers to be profitable.

Your product offers too few advantages over the alternatives.

A great amount of additional value adds up to success.

Too little additional value adds up to failure.

How can you know the value without strategic analysis?

You can see what the available alternatives are simply by looking.

You can foresee your success or failure by strategic analysis.

CHOICES:

You create success by investing in ventures where the five factors are in your favor.

Chapter 2

Going to War: Making Money

Strategy is based on economics. Though strategy was first developed in the context of war, from the very beginning it was about making a profit. As Sun Tzu said 2,500 years ago, the strategy comes down to knowing how to "make victory pay."

The time to think about these economic realities is *before* you begin a new venture. Decisions have economic consequences. In the unpredictable, uncontrolled arena of a competitive environment, you must consider the downside of your decisions. It isn't enough simply winning sales battles. You must make sure that, in the end, those sales win you a profit.

To make a profit, every business warrior must start with an analysis of the costs of the new venture. There are risks inherent in every investment of time and effort. The costs of competition can be debilitating. Money "invested" in the wrong venture is just money wasted.

Many entrepreneurs are driven by unfailing optimism, but the real costs and real rewards of a new venture are unpredictable. Because of this, you must minimize your spending to necessities if you want to be certain of making a profit.

Certain factors, such as distance and time, always increase your costs. You want to make every competitive venture pay for itself as directly and quickly as possible. Your ability to control costs is the key to a stable organization. Costs never control themselves. This is where your leadership skills are necessary.

Going to War

SUN TZU SAID:

Everything depends on your use of military philosophy. 1
Moving the army requires thousands of vehicles.
These vehicles must be loaded thousands of times.
The army must carry a huge supply of arms.
You need ten thousand acres of grain.
This results in internal and external shortages.
Any army consumes resources like an invader.
It uses up glue and paint for wood.
It requires armor for its vehicles.
People complain about the waste of a vast amount
of metal.
It will set you back when you attempt to raise tens
of thousands of troops.

ECONOMY:

Strategy teaches that the key to success is making good decisions about using limited resources.

[12]Using a huge army makes war costly to win.
Long delays create a dull army and sharp defeats.
Attacking enemy cities drains your forces.
Long violent campaigns that exhaust the nation's
resources are wrong.

Making Money

1 Everything depends on establishing the right business goals.
Moving into a new venture requires thousands of decisions.
Those decisions require the investment of many resources.
A new venture requires a good supply of products.
You need thousands of dollars in capital.
Your family and your associates will run short of money.
Undertaking a new venture consumes resources like a thief.
It consumes your time and energy.
You must defend your decisions.
People will complain about the money you've spent.
It is too expensive if you must continually rehire and retrain people to get your business off the ground.

Hiring too many employees is never profitable.
A lack of progress destroys enthusiasm.
Targeting entrenched competitors is expensive.
Drawn-out competitive battles that drain your limited resources are sure to fail.

QUICKNESS:

You cannot move quickly if you plan large, expensive ventures. This approach is deadly.

AGGRESSION:

*Going slowly
and "carefully"
is more costly
and dangerous
than moving
forward quickly.*

[16]Manage a dull army.
You will suffer sharp defeats.
Drain your forces.
Your money will be used up.
Your rivals will multiply as your army collapses
and they will begin against you.
It doesn't matter how smart you are.
You cannot get ahead by taking losses!

[23]You hear of people going to war too quickly.
Still, you won't see a skilled war that lasts a long
time.

[25]You can manage a war for a long time or you can make
your nation strong.
You can't do both.

Make no assumptions about all the dangers in using **2**
military force.
Then you won't make assumptions about the benefits of
using arms either.

SMALL IS
FAST:

*Speed is closely
connected to
size. Do not
mistake costly
size for power
and safety.*

[3]You want to make good use of war.
Do not raise troops repeatedly.
Do not carry too many supplies.
Choose to be useful to your nation.
Feed off the enemy.
Make your army carry only the provisions it
needs.

You can build a sluggish organization.
You will then lose sales consistently.
You can make expensive decisions.
Your cash cushion will then be destroyed.
Your new venture will falter and competitors will start
to take away your customers.
It doesn't matter how smart you think you are.
You can't get ahead by losing money.

MOMENTUM:

If you are not constantly making progress, you are inviting attacks on your current position.

You can sometimes go into business too quickly.
However, no good venture takes a long time to get off
the ground.

You can continue to support a losing business or become a successful entrepreneur.
You can't do both at once.

2 You can never completely insure against failure when you start
a new business.
It follows that you can never know all the opportunities your enterprise can create either.

You must make good use of your competitive skills.
Do not borrow money repeatedly.
Do not invest in too much inventory.
Choose to be valuable to your marketplace.
Take sales from your competitors.
Invest only in the items that you absolutely need.

TESTING:

Each new business venture is a test to see how quickly you can generate money from a new set of customers.

The nation impoverishes itself shipping to troops that **3** are far away.

Distant transportation is costly for hundreds of families.

Buying goods with the army nearby is also expensive.

High prices also exhaust wealth.

If you exhaust your wealth, you then quickly hollow out your military.

Military forces consume a nation's wealth entirely.

War leaves households in the former heart of the nation with nothing.

[8]War destroys hundreds of families.

Out of every ten families, war leaves only seven.

War empties the government's storehouses.

Broken armies will get rid of their horses.

They will throw down their armor, helmets, and arrows.

They will lose their swords and shields.

They will leave their wagons without oxen.

War will consume 60 percent of everything you have.

Because of this, it is the intelligent **4** commander's duty to feed off the enemy.

OPPONENTS:

Strategy demands that you deplete any resources that would naturally go to your competitors.

[2]Use a cup of the enemy's food.

It is worth twenty of your own.

Win a bushel of the enemy's feed.

It is worth twenty of your own.

3 Your customers cannot afford to pay for shipping and transportation.

Selling to distant customers is costly.

Buying products that are in short supply is also expensive.

High costs make it difficult to satisfy customers.

The high overhead costs of running a business will make you less competitive.

These costs can easily consume all your profits.

Even though you are making sales, your venture produces nothing if it isn't profitable.

Too little profit destroys thousands of new enterprises.

Eighty percent fail within the first two years.

You can invest money that you've spent a lifetime saving.

If your business fails, that investment is lost.

Your inventory becomes worthless.

Your spending in marketing and advertising is wasted.

Your equipment and offices are abandoned.

Failure can consume almost all of what you've accumulated.

4 Because of the risks, you must be certain to win the most profitable sales from the competition.

Take a dollar in profits.

It is worth twenty dollars of sales.

Sell your most profitable products.

They are worth twenty products that make nothing.

RESULTS:

Choose ventures from which you can quickly generate profits to pay for expanding those businesses.

[6]You can kill the enemy and frustrate him as well.
Take the enemy's strength from him by stealing away his money.

[8]Battle for the enemy's supply wagons.
Capture his supplies by using overwhelming force.
Reward the first who capture them.
Then change their banners and flags.
Mix them in with your own wagons to increase your supply line.
Keep your soldiers strong by providing for them.
This is what it means to beat the enemy while you grow more powerful.

Make victory in war pay for itself. 5
Avoid expensive, long campaigns.
The military commander's knowledge is the key.
It determines whether the civilian officials can govern.
It determines whether the nation's households are peaceful or a danger to the state.

♦ ♦ ♦

MAKE IT PAY:

Success is de-
fined only by its
profitability.

You can beat competitors and discourage them as well.
You must take strength away from your competitors by stealing
away their customers.

Challenge competitors for the best customers.
Concentrate your efforts on the most profitable business.
Reward your early customers for trusting you.
Advertise and promote your success with them.
Keep them with your regular customers to increase your repeat
business.
Keep your enterprise strong by making it profitable.
This is what it means to beat your competitors while growing more
competitive.

5 Make all your new ventures pay for themselves.
Avoid expensive, slow start-ups.
Your knowledge of good strategy is the key.
It determines whether or not your organization is manageable.
Strategy determines whether or not your customers are happy or a
threat to your future.

♦ ♦ ♦

ENTERPRISE:

*Choose close,
inexpensive, and
small targets.*

Chapter 3

Planning an Attack: Focusing on a Target

Strategically, "attacking" means moving into a new area. It is easy for an entrepreneur to pursue too many different, unrelated opportunities. A business warrior seeks unity and focus. Strategy defines strength not in terms of size but in terms of how focused you are. No venture can be successful trying to be all things to all people. Good strategy demands that you concentrate only on what you do best.

It doesn't matter how large or small your organization is. You need it to be united at every level. Unity creates focus, which in turn makes you powerful. The goal of strength is not just to win battles but to prevent them. Potential opponents do not challenge strong, well-focused organizations. And, of course, the most costly and destructive battles are those within an organization that has conflicting goals.

You must pursue new ventures that minimize conflict. The worst way to build an organization is to directly attack a competitor. The business warrior uses an incremental approach to success. You must set up small, focused ventures in which you have the clear advantage over any competitors. The relative strength of your competitive forces determines your basic tactics. Political divisions within an organization weaken its competitive strength.

Knowledge determines your ability to unite and concentrate your forces. It is always dangerous to miscalculate the relative strength of your organization in facing a competitor.

Planning an Attack

UNITY:

Strategy teaches that the size of an enterprise is not nearly as important as how united it is.

SUN TZU SAID:

Everyone relies on the arts of war. 1
A united nation is strong.
A divided nation is weak.
A united army is strong.
A divided army is weak.
A united force is strong.
A divided force is weak.
United men are strong.
Divided men are weak.
A united unit is strong.
A divided unit is weak.

[12]Unity works because it enables you to win every battle.
Still, this is the foolish goal of a weak leader.
Avoid battle and make the enemy's men surrender.
This is the right goal for a superior leader.

The best way to make war is to ruin the enemy's plans. 2
The next best is to disrupt alliances.
The next best is to attack the opposing army.
The worst is to attack the enemy's cities.

Focusing on a Target

THE BUSINESS WARRIOR HEARS:

1 Entrepreneurs live by their skill in competition.
A focused venture is successful.
An unfocused venture fails.
A united team wins.

FOCUS:

A divided team struggles.
A concentrated effort is powerful.
A divided effort is weak.
Well-defined target markets make you successful.
A mixed group of customers is costly to serve.
Clear-cut goals keep you on track.
Confused goals get you nowhere.

Your ability to expand your venture success-fully depends on maintaining your focus.

The more focused you are, the easier it will be to
address your business's challenges.
Still, solving problems alone doesn't create a stable business.
Avoid problems and discourage competitors.
This is the right goal for a successful business warrior.

2 It's best to go after new areas while others are still analyzing.
The next best approach is to steal away others' partners.
The next best is to go after a competitor's customers.
The worst is to target a competitor's strong points.

5This is what happens when you attack a city.
You can attempt it, but you can't finish it.
First you must make siege engines.
You need the right equipment and machinery.
It takes three months and still you cannot win.
Then you try to encircle the area.
You use three more months without making progress.
Your command still doesn't succeed and this angers you.
You then try to swarm the city.
This kills a third of your officers and men.
You are still unable to draw the enemy out of the city.
This attack is a disaster.

Make good use of war. 3
Make the enemy's troops surrender.
You can do this undertaking only minor battles.
You can draw their men out of their cities.
You can do it with small attacks.
You can destroy the men of a nation.
You must keep your campaign short.

8You must use total war, fighting with everything you have.
Never stop fighting when at war.
You can gain complete advantage.
To do this, you must plan your strategy of attack.

ATTACKS:

In classical strategy, an attack is any form of invading an opponent's territory. It is not fighting with competitors.

INTENSITY:

No matter how certain your success, you must focus intently on winning. Half-hearted efforts can always fail.

What happens when you directly attack established competitors?
You can desire the market position, but you won't get it.
First, you must break down the barriers to entering
their market.

You need to duplicate their systems and contacts.
This takes time, and still their customers don't know
you.
Then, you try to offer a superior product in every way.
After spreading yourself too thin, you don't make
money.
You get frustrated and angry.
You then spend money to win your competitors' customers.
You have to cut back on your personnel.
You are still unable to make a dent in their existing business.
This type of business venture is a disaster.

DISASTER:

Simply copying competitors' best products and marketing is a costly disaster just waiting to happen.

3 You must leverage competition to your advantage.
Let customers come to you.
You do this by offering small, special, specific benefits.
Win unhappy customers away from all competitors.
You do it by picking a niche in which to compete.
You must undermine your competitors' support.
You must quickly test ideas to see what works.

LEVERAGE:

Your real business opportunities come from your unique position within the larger environment.

You must be totally committed to the success of your
enterprise.
You must persist in trying everything to make it work.
You will find the perfect opportunity.
To do this, you must focus on growing.

¹²The rules for making war are:
If you outnumber enemy forces ten to one, surround them.
If you outnumber them five to one, attack them.
If you outnumber them two to one, divide them.
If you are equal, then find an advantageous battle.
If you are fewer, defend against them.
If you are much weaker, evade them.

¹⁹Small forces are not powerful.
However, large forces cannot catch them.

You must master command. 4
The nation must support you.

³Supporting the military makes the nation powerful.
Not supporting the military makes the nation weak.

⁵The army's position is made more difficult by politicians in
three different ways.
Ignorant of the whole army's inability to advance, they
order an advance.
Ignorant of the whole army's inability to withdraw, they
order a withdrawal.
We call this tying up the army.
Politicians don't understand the army's business.
Still, they think they can run an army.
This confuses the army's officers.

These are the rules for competing successfully:

If you are ten times bigger than your opponents, isolate a competitor.

If you are five times bigger, go directly after their business.

If you are twice as big, divide a competitor's market.

If you are the same size, specialize your product.

If you are smaller, defend a small segment.

If you are much smaller, move from niche to niche.

Small companies are not powerful.

However, large companies cannot move quickly into niches.

4 You must be able to manage your production.

Your operations must support your competitive efforts.

An enterprise is powerful when it supports competitive advances.

An enterprise is weak when it ignores its competitive situation.

Bad management creates financial problems for a business in three ways.

Regardless of the enterprise's needs, bad managers spend money freely whenever they want to.

Regardless of the enterprise's needs, bad managers refuse to invest money when it is required.

We call this hamstringing the business.

Poor managers don't understand the needs of their business.

They still think they can manage an enterprise.

Their decisions confuse the goals of the enterprise.

¹²Politicians don't know the army's chain of command.
They give the army too much freedom.
This will create distrust among the army's officers.

¹⁵The entire army becomes confused and distrusting.
This invites invasion by many different rivals.
We say correctly that disorder in an army kills victory.

You must know five things to win: **5**
Victory comes from knowing when to attack and when to avoid battle.
Victory comes from correctly using both large and small forces.
Victory comes from everyone sharing the same goals.
Victory comes from finding opportunities in problems.
Victory comes from having a capable commander and the government leaving him alone.
You must know these five things.
You then know the theory of victory.

We say: **6**
"Know yourself and know your enemy.
You will be safe in every battle.
You may know yourself but not know the enemy.
You will then lose one battle for every one you win.
You may not know yourself or the enemy.
You will then lose every battle.

† † †

Bad managers misunderstand the need for priorities.
They invest freely in too many directions.
This creates uncertainty in any venture's future.

You must not weaken an enterprise's trust in its focus and purpose.
This invites competition from many different directions.
A lack of priorities destroys your chances of success.

5 You must know five things to be a successful entrepreneur.
Success comes from knowing what needs to be done and what you can leave undone.
Success comes from focusing your limited resources on markets of the appropriate size.
Success comes from making the organization's mission clear.
Success comes from focusing on problems that others overlook.
Success comes from providing leadership and eliminating the obstacles that interfere with your ability to compete.
You must focus your business in these five ways.
You then know the concepts of building a business.

6 Strategy dictates:
Know your capabilities and those of your competitors.
If you do, you can always survive in the marketplace.
You may know your capabilities but not those of your competitors.
Then every success will lead to an eventual failure.
You can be ignorant of your abilities and your competitors'.
Then you will lose every meeting with competitors.

Chapter 4

Positioning: Establishing an Enterprise

Business warriors know how to take what they are given. According to the principles of strategy, you do not create your opportunities in the marketplace. You can only take advantage of the opportunities that others create for you. Regular people do not know how to recognize these opportunities or what to do with them. This chapter addresses those skills.

On your own, you can do no more than defend your existing position in the marketplace. Only the needs of the customers and the mistakes of your competitors can create new opportunities for you. New potential positions are stepping-stones for an entrepreneur, but the marketplace has to create those stepping-stones before you can move to them and use them.

New opportunities do not come on any schedule. You cannot plan them. Because of this, you must know how to protect your existing position until a new opportunity appears.

Recognizing a good opportunity and aiming at it are not enough. You must know how to move from your existing position to a new one. You must also know how to get rewarded from that new position once you get there.

A simple formula tells you whether or not you can succeed in winning a new position. It works by calculating who will have the most support at the place and time at which competitive decisions must be made. This depends on your ability to get what you need out of the people with whom you work.

Positioning

Sun Tzu said:

Learn from the history of successful battles. 1
Your first actions should deny victory to the enemy.
You pay attention to your enemy to find the way to win.
You alone can deny victory to the enemy.
Only your enemy can allow you to win.

6You must battle well.
You can prevent the enemy's victory.
You cannot win unless the enemy enables your victory.

9We say:
You see the opportunity for victory; you don't
create it.

Defense:

Strategy dictates that you must first make sure that your existing position is secure before moving to a new one.

Establishing an Enterprise

THE BUSINESS WARRIOR HEARS:

1 Learn from the history of successful ventures.
First, you keep your idea alive by protecting it from competitors.
You pay attention to your competitors to find opportunities.
You alone can defend your business's survival.
Only competitors can create a market opening for you.

You must invest your time and efforts well.
You can prevent the loss of existing customers.
You win new customers because competitors let you.

Strategy dictates:
You must discover your place in the market; you do not create it.

OPENINGS:

You must take advantage of opportunities in the marketplace that your competitors create for you.

You are sometimes unable to win. 2
You must then defend.
You will eventually be able to win.
You must then attack.
Defend when you have insufficient strength.
Attack when you have a surplus of strength.

7You must defend yourself well.
Save your forces and dig in.
You must attack well.
Move your forces when you have a clear advantage.

11You must always protect yourself until you can completely triumph.

Some may see how to win. 3
However, they cannot position their forces where they must.
This demonstrates limited ability.

4Some can struggle to a victory and the whole world may praise their winning.
This also demonstrates a limited ability.

6Win as easily as picking up a fallen hair.
Don't use all of your forces.
See the time to move.
Don't try to find something clever.
Hear the clap of thunder.
Don't try to hear something subtle.

2 You cannot always find a new market opportunity.
You must then concentrate on your existing customers.
You will eventually discover a market to expand into.
Then you must go after new customers.
Avoid markets that are too large for you to dominate.
Go after markets that are small enough for you to win.

You must defend existing customers well.
Conserve your resources and protect them.
You must campaign well for new customers.
Go after a new market when you have a clear opportunity.

You must conserve your resources so that you can easily win new markets when they appear.

3 You may identify new customers that you would like to win.
Yet you don't see how to contact those customers.
This shows limited ability.

You may win new customers by spending a lot of money on marketing.
This also shows limited ability.

Move into new markets effortlessly.
Avoid risking your current customers.
Wait for the time to move.
Don't try to be too clever.
Learning about opportunities is easy if you listen.
Don't imagine opportunities where you want them.

¹²Learn from the history of successful battles.
Victory goes to those who make winning easy.
A good battle is one that you will obviously win.
It doesn't take intelligence to win a reputation.
It doesn't take courage to achieve success.

¹⁷You must win your battles without effort.
Avoid difficult struggles.
Battle when your position must win.
You always win by preventing your defeat.

²¹You must engage only in winning battles.
Position yourself where you cannot lose.
Never waste an opportunity to defeat your enemy.

²⁴You win a war by first assuring yourself of victory.
Only afterward do you look for a battle.
Outmaneuver the enemy before the first battle and then
work to win.

BATTLE:

In classical strategy, battle means meeting an opponent's challenge, not necessarily a fight.

Learn from the history of successful ventures.

Success goes to those who make their success effortless.

An ideal customer is one who is inexpensive to win.

You don't have to become famous to win new markets.

You also don't have to take chances in winning customers.

You want to win new markets without effort.

Avoid highly competitive situations.

Invest all your resources when you have proven that a market works.

You always succeed if you avoid making poor decisions.

You must engage only in successful marketing campaigns.

Sell to markets that you can easily satisfy.

Never pass by an opportunity to make competitors look bad.

Build a good business by first finding the right customers.

Only then do you worry about investing resources.

Find the right customers for your business and then invest in what you need to win them.

IDENTITY:

The market needs to know who you are but only in terms of how you can easily meet its needs.

You must make good use of war. 4
Study military philosophy and the art of defense.
You can control your victory or defeat.

⁴This is the art of war:
"1.   Discuss the distances.
2.   Discuss your numbers.
3.   Discuss your calculations.
4.   Discuss your decisions.
5.   Discuss victory.

¹⁰The ground determines the distance.
The distance determines your numbers.
Your numbers determine your calculations.
Your calculations determine your decisions.
Your decisions determine your victory."

¹⁵Creating a winning war is like balancing a coin of gold
against a coin of silver.
Creating a losing war is like balancing a coin of silver
against a coin of gold.

Winning a battle is always a matter of people. 5
You pour them into battle like a flood of
water pouring into a deep gorge.
This is a matter of positioning.

✦ ✦ ✦

4 You must make use of competitive strategy.
Know your competitive goals and how to defend your markets.
You alone determine your success or failure.

This war of business requires you to:
1.   Discuss market barriers to entry.
2.   Discuss the required investment.
3.   Discuss the potential profits.
4.   Discuss your market positioning.
5.   Discuss your likelihood of success.

Customer needs determine the barriers to entry.
These barriers determine the required investment.
The investment required determines the potential profit.
The potential profit determines your market positioning.
Your market positioning determines your success.

Creating a successful market position is a matter of being the best
in one area rather than the second best in another.
Creating a losing market position is a matter of choosing areas
where you are the second-best choice.

5 Expanding your position depends on knowing customers.
You must take advantage of people's desire to
follow what others like them are doing.
This is the basis for your place in the market.

♦ ♦ ♦

Chapter 5

Momentum: Surprising With Innovations

Once you have found a place in the market, you need to build and maintain momentum. Momentum isn't created by simply doing what you have done successfully in the past. The science of strategy teaches that momentum comes from first establishing a set of expectations and then surprising others by exceeding those expectations.

Surprise, innovation, and creativity are a key ideas in strategy, but good strategy is more than just a novel idea. Unless you first establish predictability and standards, surprise is useless.

All strategy starts by relying on proven concepts and proven techniques. In business, customers want consistent results. They need predictability. They want their expectations to be satisfied. Without first establishing a baseline of standards, innovation and surprise are just chaos and confusion.

Once you establish and meet a set of expectations, you then have an infinite number of ways to create momentum through surprise and innovation. There is actually a very simple formula for coming up with a continual flow of useful ideas.

Together, the shift between standards and surprise creates momentum, but timing is also important to get the most out of this process. Momentum builds up pressure while timing releases that pressure at the right time. Timing introduces a critical amount of control into the chaos of battle. It is this control that does the most to affect people's attitudes.

Momentum

You control a large group the same as you control a few. **1**
You just divide their ranks correctly.
You fight a large army the same as you fight a small one.
You only need the right position and communication.
You may meet a large enemy army.
You must be able to sustain an enemy attack without being defeated.
You must correctly use both surprise and direct action.
Your army's position must increase your strength.
Troops flanking an enemy can smash them like eggs.
You must correctly use both strength and weakness.

It is the same in all battles. **2**
You use a direct approach to engage the enemy.
You use surprise to win.

STANDARDS:

Momentum requires developing a set of standards that customers can depend upon.

4You must use surprise for a successful invasion.
Surprise is as infinite as the weather and land.
Surprise is as inexhaustible as the flow of a river.

Surprising With Innovations

THE BUSINESS WARRIOR HEARS:

1 You control a large enterprise the same as a small one.
You need only to build the right organization.
You win large markets the same way you win small ones.
You need the right concept and marketing.
You may meet larger competitors.
You must be able to survive and keep your customers if larger opponents come after your market.
You need to use creative and standard business methods.
Your competitive strategy must give you power.
Build your business in ways that surprise competitors.
You leverage your strengths against others' weaknesses.

2 Every meeting with customers is the same.
You must establish standards to set expectations.
You must use innovation to win them.

You must use innovation to start new ventures.
Market and climate create infinite opportunities.
Innovation harnesses the flow of change in business.

INNOVATION:

Innovation of standards creates a moving target that competitors cannot easily attack.

7You can be stopped and yet recover the initiative.
You must use your days and months correctly.

9If you are defeated, you can recover.
You must use the four seasons correctly.

11There are only a few notes in the scale.
Yet you can always rearrange them.
You can never hear every song of victory.

14There are only a few basic colors.
Yet you can always mix them.
You can never see all the shades of victory.

17There are only a few flavors.
Yet you can always blend them.
You can never taste all the flavors of victory.

20You battle with momentum.
There are only a few types of surprises and direct actions.
Yet you can always vary the ones you use.
There is no limit to the ways you can win.

24Surprise and direct action give birth to each other.
They are like a circle without end.
You cannot exhaust all their possible combinations!

Surging waters flow together rapidly. 3
Their pressure washes away boulders.
This is momentum.

Today's difficulties are the seeds for tomorrow's inspiration.
Use your time to continually improve and move forward.

Not all new ideas will work at first, but you can learn.
It takes time to get innovations working.

There are only a few basic messages for selling products.
But you can rearrange messages in creative ways.
You can always inspire fresh interest on the part of customers.

There are only a few key components to any product.
But you can put them together in different ways.
You can always invent new types of products.

There are only a few basic business processes.
But you can combine the steps in new ways.
You can always find a better way to get the work done.

You build an enterprise though continual improvement.
Improvement combines innovation with proven practices.
You must combine both to make your business unique.
There are no limits to the ways you can create profits.

Innovation and proven practices are mutually dependent.
Standards inspire creativity, which inspires new standards.
Using both, you can continually improve your business.

3 One step should follow another quickly.
Continual progress can wash away any obstacle.
This is momentum.

⁴A hawk suddenly strikes a bird.
Its contact alone kills the prey.
This is timing.

⁷You must choose only winning battles.
Your momentum must be overwhelming.
Your timing must be exact.

¹⁰Your momentum is like the tension of a bent crossbow.
Your timing is like the pulling of a trigger.

War is very complicated and confusing. 4
Battle is chaotic.
Nevertheless, you must not allow chaos.

⁴War is very sloppy and messy.
Positions turn around.
Nevertheless, you must never be defeated.

⁷Chaos gives birth to control.
Fear gives birth to courage.
Weakness gives birth to strength.

MOMENTUM:

Dependable standards and constant improvement create pressure in the marketplace to buy.

¹⁰You must control chaos.
This depends on your planning.
Your men must brave their fears.
This depends on momentum.

¹⁴You have strengths and weaknesses.
These come from your position.

A customer's decision takes place in an instant.
You must make an impact to win the business.
This requires timing.

You must invest only in what wins customers.
The shift from standards to surprise must have impact.
You must time it precisely.

A change from what is expected creates tension.
You must time your surprise to create excitement.

4 Competition is always complicated and confused.
Meeting competitors is unpredictable.
Still, you must create orderly procedures.

Competition is never neat and tidy.
Situations are always changing.
Nevertheless, you need not make mistakes.

Customer confusion requires organization.
Buyer uncertainty can be turned into confidence.
Satisfying customers' expectations gives you strength.

You must organize what is confusing.
You must analyze the customer experience.
You must inspire customers to try something new.
You must combine standards with surprises.

Enterprises have both strengths and weaknesses.
No strategic position is perfect.

TIMING:

Good offers release the pressure created by momentum to give customers a reason to buy now.

¹⁶You must force the enemy to move to your advantage.
Use your position.
The enemy must follow you.
Surrender a position.
The enemy must take it.
You can offer an advantage to move him.
You can use your men to move him.
You can use your strength to hold him.

You want a successful battle. 5
To do this, you must seek momentum.
Do not just demand a good effort from your people.
You must pick good people and then give them momentum.

⁵You must create momentum.
You create it with your men during battle.
This is comparable to rolling trees and stones.
Trees and stones roll because of their shape and weight.
Offer men safety and they will stay calm.
Endanger them and they will act.
Give them a place and they will hold.
Round them up and they will march.

¹³You make your men powerful in battle with momentum.
This should be like rolling round stones down over a high,
steep cliff.
Momentum is critical.

✦ ✦ ✦

Control what your competitors do so momentum is on your side.
You do this by offering new innovations.
Your competitors will have to copy you.
You must abandon innovations when they are no longer surprising.
Your competitors will adopt them when you are done.
You can keep opponents following behind you.
Your momentum with customers forces them to keep up.
Your focus and direction keep them behind you.

5 You want to outshine the competition.
You do this by setting standards and improving on them.
Do not just ask your people to work harder.
Find a method to improve the way they work.

You need to make surprising innovations.
You must innovate the ways you handle customer contact.
You shape customers' expectations to move them.
Customers move forward when they know what to expect.
Make customers comfortable and they will stay with you.
You use surprise to challenge them to act in a new way.
Give customers a sense of belonging and they will stay with you.
Bring customers together and they will move forward.

As a business warrior, you use momentum to control customers.
You want to shape the sales process so they rush
forward without stopping.
Use surprising innovations.

✦ ✦ ✦

Chapter 6

Weakness and Strength: Seeing Openings

Strategy teaches you not to try to force your way forward.
Instead, you look for openings that make progress easy. To see
openings, you need to understand two opposing but complementary concepts. The first concept is "weakness," but it also
means needs, emptiness, and a lack of resources. The second
concept is "strength," but it also means satisfaction, fullness,
and a surplus of resources. Together these two ideas describe a
cycle that creates and fills openings naturally.

You have probably heard that nature abhors a vacuum. This is
true not only in physics but in the science of strategy as well. Weak,
empty, and needy conditions cry out to be satisfied, and, in the
natural course of things, they are satisfied. In strategy, these weakness states are considered "openings" or opportunities.

However, there is a powerful psychological force that prevents
people from seeing these opportunities. People see weakness and
neediness as problems. They are frightened by emptiness. Most
people prefer to follow the crowd. Most people cannot see opportunities because they need someone to lead the way.

Those who are willing to break away from the crowd are those
who have the courage to embrace weakness and emptiness. Strategy
teaches that by doing so you become strong. However, the science
of strategy also teaches that strength, fullness, and satisfaction are
only temporary states. They naturally revert to back to weakness,
emptiness, and neediness over time.

Weakness and Strength

SUN TZU SAID:

Always arrive first to the empty battlefield to await the 1
enemy at your leisure.
After the battleground is occupied and you hurry to it, battling is more difficult.

3You want a successful battle.
Move your men, but not into opposing forces.

5You can make the enemy come to you.
Offer him an advantage.
You can make the enemy avoid coming to you.
Threaten him with danger.

9When the enemy is fresh, you can tire him.
When he is well fed, you can starve him.
When he is relaxed, you can move him.

WEAKNESS:

*Competitors'
weaknesses
arise naturally
from unsatisfied
customer needs.
Needs create
opportunities.*

Seeing Openings

THE BUSINESS WARRIOR HEARS:

1 You want to see openings in the market and fill them before opponents recognize them.
Rushing into marketplaces that are already crowded makes beating competitors difficult.

You want all your moves to be successful.
Go after new markets but not ones that are already crowded.

You can entice competitors into new markets to help develop them.
Let everyone know the opportunity.
You can scare others away from a market to protect it.
Let everyone know the problems.

You can exhaust a fresh opponent.
You can drain a rich opponent.
You can push around a wealthy opponent.

STRENGTHS:

All competitors have areas of strength that make some markets easier for them than others.

Leave any place without haste. 2
Hurry to where you are unexpected.
You can easily march hundreds of miles without tiring.
To do so, travel through areas that are deserted.
You must take whatever you attack.
Attack when there is no defense.
You must have walls to defend.
Defend where it is impossible to attack.

AVOIDANCE:

Success depends upon avoiding competitive challenges while you move to develop better positions.

⁹Be skilled in attacking.
Give the enemy no idea where to defend.

¹¹Be skillful in your defense.
Give the enemy no idea where to attack.

Be subtle! Be subtle! 3
Arrive without any clear formation.
Ghostly! Ghostly!
Arrive without a sound.
You must use all your skill to control the enemy's decisions.

⁶Advance where he can't defend.
Charge through his openings.
Withdraw where the enemy cannot chase you.
Move quickly so that he cannot catch you.

2 Abandon less profitable products and services gradually.
Target new areas that are being overlooked.
You can completely reposition your enterprise with ease.
To do so, you must explore markets where there is no competition.
You must win new customers when you go after them.
Work with customers whose needs are unsatisfied.
You must create barriers to entry in those markets.
Leave no needs for your competitors to satisfy.

Be skilled in moving into new markets.
Search out problems that others have left unresolved.

Be skilled in protecting your markets.
Provide solutions that have no weaknesses.

> **SPECIALIZE:**
>
> *Focus your marketing on products and market positions that are difficult for competitors to duplicate.*

3 Change market positions without others noticing.
Do not let competitors know your plan.
Keep quiet about what you are doing.
Move into new markets quietly.
Communicate to customers directly so your competitors can't react.

Sell to markets where competitors are handicapped.
Aggressively fill the gaps that competitors leave.
Put yourself into market niches where there are barriers to entry.
Change your offerings so competitors cannot copy you.

Always pick your own customers.

[10]Always pick your own battles.
The enemy can hide behind high walls and deep trenches.
Do not try to win by battling him directly.
Instead, attack a place that he must recapture.
Avoid the battles that you don't want.
You can divide the ground and yet defend it.
Don't give the enemy anything to win.
Divert him by coming to where you defend.

Make other men take a position while you take none. 4
Then focus your forces where the enemy divides his forces.
Where you focus, you unite your forces.
When the enemy divides, he creates many small groups.
You want your large group to attack one of his small ones.
Then you have many men where the enemy has but a few.
Your larger force can overwhelm his smaller one.
Then go on to the next small enemy group.
You can take them one at a time.

You must keep the place that you have chosen as a 5
battleground a secret.
The enemy must not know.
Force the enemy to prepare his defense in many places.
You want the enemy to defend many places.
Then you can choose where to fight.
His forces will be weak there.

SECRECY:

You cannot exploit the weakness of your opponents if everyone knows what you are doing.

Your competitors can be well entrenched in their markets.
You cannot beat them by going after these markets directly.
Instead, find the customers that they are serving poorly.
Battling over customers is never profitable.
You can divide the market to create your own segment.
Do not leave needs in your market for others to address.
Distract competitors from coming after your customers.

4 Know what competitors do well before building your enterprise.
Focus your venture on gaps in competing businesses.
When you focus, you concentrate your resources.
Where competitors divide their attention, they create openings.
You must focus all your efforts into areas competitors serve poorly.
You put a lot of resources into areas where others have put little.
You can easily do a better job there than your competitors can.
You can then move on to the next opening in the market.
Tackle customer problems one at a time.

5 You must keep your future direction a secret from your competitors.
Don't give your competitors any ideas.
Your opponents have many different areas in which they
can invest their resources.
You want them to spread themselves too thin.
You can then choose the opening that you want.
You target customers that the opponent has ignored.

If competitors focus on price, they sacrifice quality.

ADAPTABILITY:

Strength does not come from size and money. It comes from adapting to an opponent's weaknesses.

7If he reinforces his front lines, he depletes his rear.
If he reinforces his rear, he depletes his front.
If he reinforces his right flank, he depletes his left.
If he reinforces his left flank, he depletes his right.
Without knowing the place of attack, he cannot
prepare.
Without knowing the right place, he will be weak
everywhere.

WEAK POINTS:

*You must see
a competitor's
most serious
weak points
and focus your
strengths on
exploiting them.*

13The enemy has weak points.
Prepare your men against them.
He has strong points.
Make his men prepare themselves against you.

You must know the battleground. 6
You must know the time of battle.
You can then travel a thousand miles and still win the battle.

4The enemy should not know the battleground.
He shouldn't know the time of battle.
His left flank will be unable to support his right.
His right will be unable to support his left.
His front lines will be unable to support his rear.
His rear will be unable to support his front.
His support is distant even if it is only ten miles away.
What unknown place can be close?

12You control the balance of forces.
The enemy may have many men but they are superfluous.
How can they help him to victory?

If they focus on quality, they are vulnerable on price.

If they focus on speed, they lack accuracy.

If they focus on accuracy, they lose on speed.

Not focusing on your specialty, they leave an opening for you.

If they attempt everything, they leave openings everywhere.

NEEDS:

The marketplace has an infinite number of needs. You must choose those that you can best address.

All customers have unmet needs.

Create your business to address those needs.

Competitors offer specific solutions.

They cannot satisfy every type of customer.

6 You must choose where to compete.

You must choose when to move into new markets.

Markets that seem difficult are easy when you control the situation.

Your competitors must not understand the opening.

They should not foresee your moves.

If competitors work globally, you focus locally.

If they offer popular products, you can offer unique ones.

If they deal in large volumes, you can offer small ones.

If they use standard terms, you can create special ones.

They will continually overlook opportunities under their nose.

What unknown challenge can be easy?

You control how much competition you have.

Competitors may be bigger, but they are focused elsewhere.

How can their size hurt you?

Strategy dictates:

[15]We say:
You must let victory happen.

[17]The enemy may have many men.
You can still control him without a struggle.

When you form your strategy, know the strengths and 7
weaknesses of your plan.
When you execute a plan, know how to manage both action
and inaction.
When you take a position, know the deadly and the winning
grounds.
When you enter into battle, know when you have too many
or too few men.

[5]Use your position as your war's centerpiece.
Arrive at the battle without a formation.
Don't take a position in advance.
Then even the best spies can't report it.
Even the wisest general cannot plan to counter you.
Take a position where you can triumph using superior numbers.
Keep opposing forces ignorant.
Everyone should learn your location after your position has
given you success.
No one should know how your location gives you a winning
position.
Make a successful battle one from which the enemy cannot
recover.
You must continually adjust your position to his position.

You must let your venture succeed.

Competitors may be much bigger than you are.
You beat them by choosing where and when you compete.

7 When you analyze your position, know your strengths and weaknesses.
When you look to advance your position, know what needs to be done and what does not.
When you pick customers, know which people are satisfied and which people have needs.
When you choose to compete, know where you have the advantage and where you are overmatched.

Use your existing position as the fulcrum for future moves.
Move into new markets ready to adapt to the situation.
Do not plan what you are going to do.
You can keep potential customers and competitors guessing.
If you don't have a plan, no one can frustrate you.
Commit only where your strengths meet competitors' weaknesses.
Work where your competitors are ignorant.
Competitors should only learn about your enterprise when you have won away customers.
Competitors should not understand how your position is winning customers.
Make sure that competitors cannot win their customers back from you.
Move to block every move that competitors try to make.

8 You must remain flexible in positioning a business.

Manage your military position like water. 8
Water takes every shape.
It avoids the high and moves to the low.
Your war can take any shape.
It must avoid the strong and strike the weak.
Water follows the shape of the land that directs its flow.
Your forces follow the enemy, who determines how you win.

[8]Make war without a standard approach.
Water has no consistent shape.
If you follow the enemy's shifts and changes, you can always
find a way to win.
We call this shadowing.

[12]Start five different campaigns without a firm rule for victory.
Use all four seasons without a consistent position.
Your timing must be sudden.
A few weeks determine your failure or success.

ADJUSTMENT:

*Continuously
adjust to continu-
ous change.*

Any operation can work in many different ways.
You avoid what is difficult and do what is easy.
Your enterprise can take any shape.
You must avoid strong competitors and address customers' needs.
Sales should shape your venture and determine its direction.
You discover the right customers and let them guide your actions.

You must avoid rigid business plans.
Good ideas have no consistent shape.
Keep in touch with what your competitors are doing, and you will find an opening.
Follow what they do but do not duplicate it.

Different ventures call for different methods to succeed.
Different climates require flexibility in your strategic approach.
You must always act quickly.
You will fail if you don't take advantage of openings right away.

✦ ✦ ✦

URGENCY:

Entrepreneurs must make prof- its quickly.

Chapter 7

Armed Conflict: Winning Sales

Every sale arises out of conflict. Customers have to choose how to spend their money among conflicting options. Every dollar spent on one choice is one less dollar to spend on another choice. In every sale, the desire for gain battles against the fear of loss. Success in business depends on minimizing this sense of conflict rather than exacerbating it. However, in the end, to survive as an entrepreneur, you must win these conflicts when they are forced upon you.

A complete sales process follows the four-step strategic cycle. You listen to customers. You aim at their desires. You move to get their agreement. You claim to close the deal. In this chapter, we are concerned with only one part of that process. However, you move to get customers' agreement, even when they don't agree with you initially.

Business warriors do not take sales lightly. Income is the life blood of every enterprise. Your actions can destroy your chance of making a sale if you rush into the process without proper preparation. The secret of successful sales is controlling potential customers' perceptions during the process.

Communication is the key. You have to speak the customers' language in a way that allows them to hear you. You have to pick the right time and place to make contact to control the situation. There are a number of mistakes that most people make during sales battles that you must learn how to avoid.

Armed Conflict

Sun Tzu said:

Everyone uses the arts of war. 1
You accept orders from the government.
Then you assemble your army.
You organize your men and build camps.
You must avoid disasters from armed conflict.

⁶Seeking armed conflict can be disastrous.
Because of this, a detour can be the shortest path.
Because of this, problems can become opportunities.

CONFLICT:

Strategy teaches that conflict is always costly so it is ideally avoided whenever possible.

⁹Use an indirect route as your highway.
Use the search for advantage to guide you.
When you fall behind, you must catch up.
When you get ahead, you must wait.
You must know the detour that most directly
accomplishes your plan.

¹⁴Undertake armed conflict when you have an
advantage.
Seeking armed conflict for its own sake is dangerous.

Winning Sales

THE BUSINESS WARRIOR HEARS:

1 Every entrepreneur tries to use strategy.
It all starts with having a mission.
You then put together your resources.
You organize your operation and choose a location.
You must then avoid mistakes in sales contact.

Exaggerating the conflicts in the sales process is disastrous.
Because of this, you look for ways around objections.
Your opportunities come from customers' problems.

Getting money is a by-product of the sales process.
You follow the customers' lead to understand their needs.
When they get ahead of you, you must catch up.
When you get ahead of them, you must slow down.
You must know how to control the process of the sale
without seeming to be in control.

You can only insist on a decision from the customer
when all the advantages are on your side.
Insisting on a decision just because you want to close
the sale is disastrous.

DETOUR:

The shortest path to getting what you want is giving other people what they want.

You can build up an army to fight for an advantage. 2
Then you won't catch the enemy.
You can force your army to go fight for an advantage.
Then you abandon your heavy supply wagons.

⁵You keep only your armor and hurry after the enemy.
You avoid stopping day or night.
You use many roads at the same time.
You go hundreds of miles to fight for an advantage.
Then the enemy catches your commanders and your army.
Your strong soldiers get there first.
Your weaker soldiers follow behind.
Using this approach, only one in ten will arrive.
You can try to go fifty miles to fight for an advantage.
Then your commanders and army will stumble.
Using this method, only half of your soldiers will make it.
You can try to go thirty miles to fight for an advantage.
Then only two out of three get there.

¹⁸If you make your army travel without good
supply lines, your army will die.
Without supplies and food, your army will die.
If you don't save the harvest, your army will die.

FIGHTING:

You do not create opportunities by fighting for them. The use of force without strategy is wasted effort.

2 You can fight with people about why they should buy.
You will never win customers that way.
You can pressure customers to see the value in what you are selling.
You then fail to learn what they need.

You can try to rush the customer into making a decision.
You can pressure him or her to buy.
You can try many different arguments at the same time.
You can spend all your time praising your product.
The customer can still reject your product and approach.
You think you are winning the sale at first.
Over time the customer will ignore you.
Only a small fraction of your effort is useful.
You can try less pressure in the sales process.
You will still lose sales that you should have made.
You waste half your efforts.
You can press for sales that are almost closed.
That pressure will lose you one out of three sales.

You can try to shortcut the sales process, but your venture will fail.
Without the proper information, your venture will fail.
Without happy customers, your venture will fail.

SHORTCUTS:

Every step in the sales process is necessary. Leaving out a step is like a bridge with a missing span.

²¹Do not let any of your potential enemies know what you are planning.

Still, you must not hesitate to form alliances.

You must know the mountains and forests.

You must know where the obstructions are.

You must know where the marshes are.

If you don't, you cannot move the army.

If you don't, you must use local guides.

If you don't, you can't take advantage of the terrain.

You make war using a deceptive position. 3

If you use deception, then you can move.

Using deception, you can upset the enemy and change the situation.

You can move as quickly as the wind.

You can rise like the forest.

You can invade and plunder like fire.

You can stay as motionless as a mountain.

You can be as mysterious as the fog.

You can strike like sounding thunder.

DECEPTION:

Success comes from controlling people's perceptions by shaping the way situations must appear to them.

¹⁰Divide your troops to plunder the villages.

When on open ground, dividing is an advantage.

Don't worry about organization; just move.

Be the first to find a new route that leads directly to a winning plan.

This is how you are successful at armed conflict.

Instead, you must say only what is absolutely needed about what you are selling.

You must become your customers' partner in the process.

You must know your customers' needs.

You must know where their problems are.

You must avoid getting bogged down in trivialities.

You must be knowledgeable to make the sale.

You must rely on your understanding of your customers.

You must take advantage of your customers' thinking.

3 You must disguise your desire to make a sale.
If customers don't fight you, you can make progress.

You uncover their problems, understand them, and use the situation.

To make sales, you must think on your feet.

You must be forthright and determined.

You must be courageous and hungry.

You must be quiet and patient.

You must keep your goals to yourself.

You must be brave enough to ask for the sale.

Come at customers' needs from different directions.

Open-minded customers like a variety of reasons.

Get them to agree with any reason to buy and move on.

Find a new reason to buy that the customer hasn't thought of before.

This is how you are successful at making sales.

AGREEMENT:

You cannot appear to sell when getting agreement, but this makes it the most powerful selling tool.

Military experience says: 4
"You can speak, but you will not be heard.
You must use gongs and drums.
You cannot really see your forces just by looking.
You must use banners and flags."

⁶You must master gongs, drums, banners and flags.
Place people as a single unit where they can all see and hear.
You must unite them as one.
Then the brave cannot advance alone.
The fearful cannot withdraw alone.
You must force them to act as a group.

¹²In night battles, you must use numerous fires and drums.
In day battles, you must use many banners and flags.
You must position your people to control what they see and
hear.

You control your army by controlling its morale. 5
As a general, you must be able to control emotions.

³In the morning, a person's energy is high.
During the day, it fades.
By evening, a person's thoughts turn to home.
You must use your troops wisely.
Avoid the enemy's high spirits.
Strike when his men are lazy and want to go home.
This is how you master energy.

4 Competitive strategy dictates:
"Words alone are not enough.
Use pictures and charts.
Demonstrating is not enough.
Use showmanship and magic."

Use pictures, props, and showmanship to get people's attention.
Make sure customers have the time and inclination to hear you.
Tie your sales presentation together.
Don't offer novel concepts alone.
Tie them together with comfortable, familiar ideas.
Every word must amplify a single, clear message.

When you are unknown, you must excite curiosity and interest.
If you are better known, you still must keep it interesting.
You must offer a product that everyone can understand and
appreciate.

5 You must get your customers' attention.
As a salesperson, you must use emotion.

In the morning, customer resistance is high.
During the day, it fades.
By evening, customers want to go home.
You must use your time wisely.
Avoid tough resistance.
Close when resistance fades and customers want to go home.
This is how you master energy.

¹⁰Use discipline to await the chaos of battle.
Keep relaxed to await a crisis.
This is how you master emotion.

¹³Stay close to home to await a distant enemy.
Stay comfortable to await the weary enemy.
Stay well fed to await the hungry enemy.
This is how you master power.

Don't entice the enemy when his ranks are orderly. 6
You must not attack when his formations are solid.
This is how you master adaptation.

⁴You must follow these military rules.
Do not take a position facing the high ground.
Do not oppose those with their backs to the wall.
Do not follow those who pretend to flee.
Do not attack the enemy's strongest men.
Do not swallow the enemy's bait.
Do not block an army that is heading home.
Leave an escape outlet for a surrounded army.
Do not press a desperate foe.
This is how you use military skills.

✦ ✦ ✦

EMOTION:

Strategy teaches that emotion is the key to action. If you control emotions, you control actions.

Keep organized when the customer is confused.
Stay quiet while the customer blows off steam.
This is how you master your feelings.

Stick to your point and wait for others to respond.
Stay friendly as you wear down the customer's resistance.
You will be successful if you serve the needs of others.
This is how you master persuasion.

6 Do not create organized resistance.
Do not attack firmly held beliefs.
This is how you master adaptation.

You must follow these sales rules.
Do not take a position against strong feelings.
Do not fight an argument based on a lack of alternatives.
Do not accept those who only pretend to agree.
Do not attack your strongest competition.
Do not believe everything the customer tells you.
Do not argue with a customer who agrees with you.
Give the customer an agreeable alternative.
Do not press the customer too hard for a decision.
These are the rules of selling.

✦ ✦ ✦

MESSAGE:

Your message must not be how great you or your products are, but how you can make your customers great.

Chapter 8

Adaptability: Adjusting to Customers

This chapter introduces the second part of the book. Thus far, we have dealt with the basic principles of strategy. This next section covers the rules for responding appropriately to changing conditions. Remember, competitive environments are dynamic. Customers' attitudes can change in a moment. Successful strategies must constantly adjust to customers' changing needs.

The following three chapters cover long lists of specific situations, how to recognize them, and how to respond to them. This chapter is meant only as a general introduction to the concept of adaptability itself.

Strategic adaptability doesn't mean that you can do whatever seems like a good idea. You have to respond appropriately to the situation. As long as you respond appropriately, you can constantly adapt your methods without being inconsistent in your results.

If you understand the changing situation better than your competitors, you can actually use the dynamics of competitive situations to control your opponents' behavior. Opponents are unpredictable. If you want to defend your position, you have to learn to use the situation to control them.

Mistakes in responding to the situation usually arise from flaws in character. The five weaknesses of entrepreneurs result not from a lack of character but usually from an excess of emotion, causing them to respond to unexpected changes by making matters worse.

Adaptability

Sᴜɴ Tᴢᴜ ꜱᴀɪᴅ:

Everyone uses the arts of war. 1
As a general, you get your orders from the government.
You gather your troops.
On dangerous ground, you must not camp.
Where the roads intersect, you must join your allies.
When an area is cut off, you must not delay in it.
When you are surrounded, you must scheme.
In a life-or-death situation, you must battle.
There are roads that you must not take.
There are armies that you must not fight.
There are strongholds that you must not attack.
There are positions that you must not defend.
There are government commands that must not be
obeyed.

Aᴅᴀᴘᴛᴀʙɪʟɪᴛʏ:

Adaptability doesn't mean doing what you want. It means knowing the appropriate response to the situation.

[14]Military leaders must be experts in knowing how
to adapt to find an advantage.
This will teach you the use of war.

Adjusting to Customers

1 Entrepreneurs always try to think competitively.
You get your direction from your mission.
You put together your resources.
When you have invested heavily, you cannot rest on your laurels.
When you need help, you must find partners.
When customers reject you, you must not give up.
When you are outmaneuvered, you must be creative.
When you are in a desperate situation, you risk it all.
There are products and services you should not sell.
There are customers that you don't want.
There are competitors that you cannot challenge.
There are mistakes that you must not defend.
There are times to ignore standard operating procedures.

You must become an expert at knowing how to adapt your practices to make a venture succeed.
Adapting to customers is the key to business success.

RESILIENCE:

You become more resilient when you see that no situation is good or bad in itself. All that matters is your response.

[16]Some commanders are not good at making adjustments to find an advantage.
They can know the shape of the terrain.
Still, they cannot find an advantageous position.

[19]Some military commanders do not know how to adjust their methods.
They can find an advantageous position.
Still, they cannot use their men effectively.

You must be creative in your planning. 2
You must adapt to your opportunities and weaknesses.
You can use a variety of approaches and still have a consistent result.
You must adjust to a variety of problems and consistently solve them.

You can deter your potential enemy by using his 3 weaknesses against him.
You can keep your potential enemy's army busy by giving it work to do.
You can rush your potential enemy by offering him an advantageous position.

PLANNING:

Planning does not mean creating a rigid to-do list, but constantly rethinking what the situation demands.

Some entrepreneurs are unable to change their direction to make customers happy.
They might know what the customer desires.
Still, they cannot develop a product that customers want.

Some entrepreneurs do not know how to adjust their business practices.
They know what their customers want.
Still, they are unable to present it to them effectively.

2 You must be inventive in your product strategy.
You must see where customers' needs create openings for you.
You can offer different products at different times and still consistently win sales.
Every situation offers unique challenges, but you can always find good solutions.

3 You can hold customers by using their needs and desires against them.
You can engage your customers by giving them an interesting problem to solve.
You can control the pace of sales by giving customers a reason to buy now.

CHANGE:

Business warriors embrace change so that they can respond more quickly than their competitors.

You must make use of war. 4
Do not trust that the enemy isn't coming.
Trust your readiness to meet him.
Do not trust that the enemy won't attack.
Rely only on your ability to pick a place that the enemy can't
attack.

You can exploit five different faults in a leader. 5
If he is willing to die, you can kill him.
If he wants to survive, you can capture him.
He may have a quick temper.
You can then provoke him with insults.
If he has a delicate sense of honor, you can disgrace him.
If he loves his people, you can create problems for him.
In every situation, look for these five weaknesses.
They are common faults in commanders.
They always lead to military disaster.

[11]To overturn an army, you must kill its general.
To do this, you must use these five weaknesses.
You must always look for them.

PREPARATION:

*The battlefield
always favors
those who are
the most men-
tally prepared
for things not
going according
to plan.*

♦ ♦ ♦

4 You must use your resources carefully.
Don't assume that customers won't use competitors against you.
Instead, be ready to meet any competitive challenges.
Do not trust that customers won't criticize your company.
Instead, you should position your company so that customers can't easily criticize it.

5 Entrepreneurs commonly have five character flaws.
If they are willing to go out of business, they will go out of business.
If they lack courage, they will be cowed by competition.
They can get upset too easily.
They can be too sensitive to rejection.
If they cannot take criticism, they will ignore problems.
If they love their employees, they will tolerate poor behavior.
In every situation, beware of these five overreactions.
They are the common failures of entrepreneurs.
They can lead you to disaster in any enterprise.

These weaknesses can destroy you and your business.
You must exploit these weaknesses in competitors.
You must recognize these flaws in yourself and others.

♦ ♦ ♦

FLAWS:

The unexpected changes in the dynamic competitive environment prey on the emotional weaknesses of entrepreneurs.

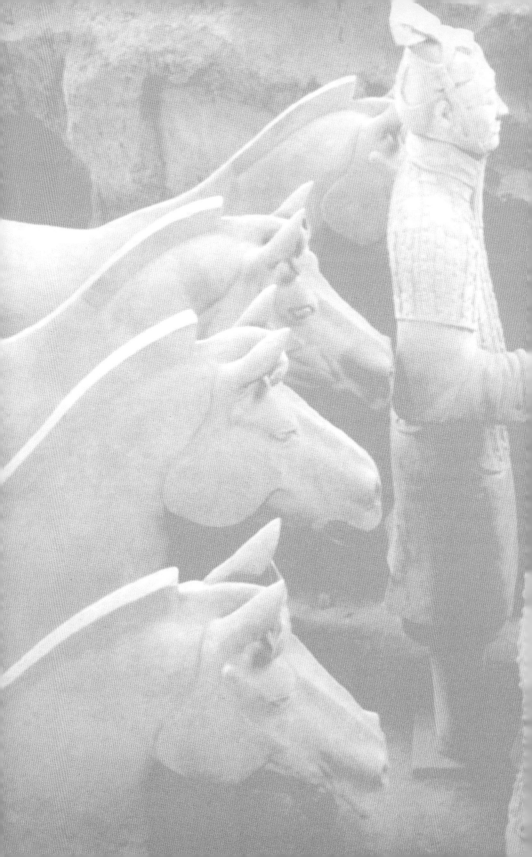

Chapter 9

Armed March: Mastering Competitors

Entrepreneurship means growing the enterprise. As you move your organization into new territory, you are going to encounter new challenges from competitors. This detailed chapter addresses how you must respond to the specific nature of those challenges. When it comes to mastering your competition, the devil is in the details. You must know how to recognize each specific situation and respond appropriately.

When meeting competitors, the first thing that you must take into consideration is the type of marketplace you are in. Classical strategy describes four general categories that affect your position in relation to that of the competition. Some markets are uneven. Others are fast-changing. Some are uncertain. And a few are broad, stable, and solid. Each type has its own rules.

When meeting competitors, you always want to control the high ground. This gets the forces of the marketplace on your side and establishes a good view of the market. Seasonal and hidden dangers are inherent in exploring new territory. You need to see what is happening to recognize various signs in the environment and interpret them correctly.

The most detailed lessons of this chapter deal with understanding the position of your competitors. You can only determine the conditions and intentions of your opponents by interpreting their behavior. You have to recognize when you have gone as far as you can in a new competitive arena and how you can regroup.

Armed March

Sun Tzu said:

Anyone moving an army must adjust to the enemy. 1
When caught in the mountains, rely on their valleys.
Position yourself on the heights facing the sun.
To win your battles, never attack uphill.
This is how you position your army in the mountains.

⁶When water blocks you, keep far away from it.
Let the invader cross the river and wait for him.
Do not meet him in midstream.
Wait for him to get half his forces across and then
take advantage of the situation.

¹⁰You need to be able to battle.
You can't do that if you are caught in water when
you meet an invader.
Position yourself upstream, facing the sun.
Never face against the current.
Always position your army upstream when near
the water.

Terrain:

*Strategy teaches
that all terrains
have a different
form and these
forms dictate
how you must
respond.*

Mastering Competitors

1 In every venture, you must meet competitive challenges.
When large customers dominate a market, rely on small customers.
Establish a visible position with a few larger customers.
Never struggle with the larger accounts for their business.
This is how you grow your business in uneven marketplaces.

When parts of your market are changing rapidly, avoid them.
Wait for your competitors to get embroiled in market changes.
Don't challenge competitors by involving yourself.
Wait until market changes divide your opponents and
then use their division as an opportunity.

You need to be able to use your resources.
You can't if you are wrestling with changes when you
meet the competition.
Get ahead of the trends and keep yourself visible.
Never fight against market changes.
Always leverage the forces of change when you are in a
fast-changing market.

MARKETS:

*Markets have
different forms
just like any
ground. They
can be uneven,
fluid, uncertain,
or solid.*

¹⁵You may have to move across marshes.
Move through them quickly without stopping.
You may meet the enemy in the middle of a marsh.
You must keep on the water grasses.
Keep your back to a clump of trees.
This is how you position your army in a marsh.

²¹On a level plateau, take a position that you can change.
Keep the higher ground on your right and to the rear.
Keep danger in front of you and safety behind.
This is how you position yourself on a level plateau.

²⁵You can find an advantage in all four of these situations.
Learn from the great emperor who used positioning to conquer his four rivals.

Armies are stronger on high ground and weaker on low. 2
They are better camping on sunny southern hillsides than
on shady northern ones.
Provide for your army's health and place men correctly.
Your army will be free from disease.
Done correctly, this means victory.

⁶You must sometimes defend on a hill or riverbank.
You must keep on the south side in the sun.
Keep the uphill slope at your right rear.

⁹This will give the advantage to your army.
It will always give you a position of strength.

You find yourself in unstable customer markets.
Get out of these markets as quickly as you can.
You may meet competitive challenges in uncertain conditions.
When you do, keep the parts of the market you know the best.
Protect yourself from getting pushed into more chaotic situations.
This is how you meet competitors in unstable markets.

When markets are broad, keep your operations and products flexible.
Base your position on the most profitable, visible products.
Stay in front of the competition and avoid missteps.
This is how you meet competitors in broad markets.

You can meet the competition in any of these four markets.
Learn from successful entrepreneurs who have continually out-maneuvered their competition.

2 Enterprises are stronger selling quality rather than price.
It is healthier to establish highly visible, transparent operations
rather than shady, questionable ones.
Put employees and partners in a good position to keep them honest.
Your venture must be proud of its products.
Doing this correctly will beat the competition.

Sometimes you must defend a higher price.
Make the better value of your product known.
You always want to offer the best value for the price.

Honesty will always give an advantage to your operation.
Market strength is built on trust and dependability.

Stop the march when the rain swells the river into rapids. 3
You may want to ford the river.
Wait until it subsides.

4All regions can have seasonal mountain streams that can
cut you off.
There are seasonal lakes.
There are seasonal blockages.
There are seasonal jungles.
There are seasonal floods.
There are seasonal fissures.
Get away from all these quickly.
Do not get close to them.
Keep them at a distance.
Maneuver the enemy close to them.
Position yourself facing these dangers.
Push the enemy back into them.

16Danger can hide on your army's flank.
There are reservoirs and lakes.
There are reeds and thickets.
There are mountain woods.
Their dense vegetation provides a hiding place.
You must cautiously search through them.
They can always hide an ambush.

SEASONS:

*The changing
climate part of
every strategic
position means
that positions
continually
change.*

3 You must stabilize your position when a market is in turmoil.
You may want to advance your position.
Wait until change in your marketplace quiets down.

All enterprises have temporary limits that restrict what they can do
in their marketplace.
There are resource limitations.
There are expense limitations.
There are information limitations.
There are legal limitations.
There are span-of-control limitations.
Do not test these limitations.
Leave yourself plenty of room for error.
Give your operations a large margin of safety.
Force your competitors to their limits.
Keep your eye on your limitations.
Let your competitors ignore them.

Problems can hide in the shadows of your business.
Fashion can become fad.
Variety can become confusion.
You may not see that you are going against the trends.
The confusion of markets can always surprise you.
You must continually analyze your market position.
You do not want to be surprised.

PATIENCE:

Market changes endanger campaigns only if you rush into them without realizing what is happening.

Sometimes, the enemy is close by but remains calm. 4
Expect to find him in a natural stronghold.
Other times he remains at a distance but provokes battle.
He wants you to attack him.

5He sometimes shifts the position of his camp.
He is looking for an advantageous position.

7The trees in the forest move.
Expect that the enemy is coming.
The tall grasses obstruct your view.
Be suspicious.

11The birds take flight.
Expect that the enemy is hiding.
Animals startle.
Expect an ambush.

15Notice the dust.
It sometimes rises high in a straight line.
Vehicles are coming.
The dust appears low in a wide band.
Foot soldiers are coming.
The dust seems scattered in different areas.
The enemy is collecting firewood.
Any dust is light and settling down.
The enemy is setting up camp.

COMPETITION:

Competition is part of the competitive environment and must be analyzed as part of that environment.

4 Competitors sell to your marketplace but they are quiet.
You should expect that they have a solid position.
Competitors distance their products from yours but challenge you.
They want you to copy them.

A competitor's position seems to invite attack.
Always expect that your opponent has a secret advantage.

The leaders in a marketplace begin to shift.
Expect that a competitor is active.
A market can be difficult to evaluate.
Expect to be surprised once you are in it.

Your market guides suddenly disappear.
Suspect that a competitor is getting close to them.
Buyers are suddenly nervous.
A competitor is undercutting you.

Ask for information about competitors.
News can be direct and straightforward.
Expect a quick competitive challenge.
News can come from everywhere in the market.
This means that competitors have many active salespeople.
News of competitors is scattered in different areas.
This means that they are developing resources.
News of competitors becomes rarer and rarer.
This means that they staying where they are.

EVALUATION:

Competitors don't tell you what they are planning, so you must judge them by what you see in the market.

Your enemy speaks humbly while building up forces. 5
He is planning to advance.

³The enemy talks aggressively and pushes as if to advance.
He is planning to retreat.

⁵Small vehicles exit his camp first.
They move the army's flanks.
They are forming a battle line.

⁸Your enemy tries to sue for peace but without offering a
treaty.
He is plotting.

¹⁰Your enemy's men run to leave and yet form ranks.
You should expect action.

¹²Half his army advances and the other half retreats.
He is luring you.

¹⁴Your enemy plans to fight but his men just stand there.
They are starving.

¹⁶Those who draw water drink it first.
They are thirsty.

¹⁸Your enemy sees an advantage but does not advance.
His men are tired.

5 Competitors talk cooperation but beef up sales and marketing.
They are coming after you.

Competitors say they want your market but do not campaign.
Expect them to go elsewhere.

Competitors move into your market quickly.
They support advertising with a sales effort.
They are serious about winning your customers.

Competitors want to discuss an agreement but without making a
real commitment.
Expect them to mislead you.

Competitors withdraw but reorganize their sales force.
Expect them to come back again.

Competitors send mixed signals about challenging you.
They want you to make the first move.

Competitors truly need your marketplace, but they are idle.
Their organization is out of resources.

Competitors offer incentives for cash payment from customers.
They are short of money.

Competitors have more opportunity but don't take advantage of it.
They are too busy to do more.

²⁰Birds gather.
Your enemy has abandoned his camp.

²²Your enemy's soldiers call in the night.
They are afraid.

²⁴Your enemy's army is raucous.
The men do not take their commander seriously.

²⁶Your enemy's banners and flags shift.
Order is breaking down.

²⁸Your enemy's officers are irritable.
They are exhausted.

JUDGMENT:

You best judge your competitors' situation by what they and their employees do rather than what they say.

³⁰Your enemy's men kill their horses for meat.
They are out of provisions.

³²They don't put their pots away or return to their tents.
They are desperate.

³⁴Enemy troops appear sincere and agreeable.
But their men are slow to speak to each other.
They are no longer united.

³⁷Your enemy offers too many incentives to his men.
He is in trouble.

Consultants come to you.
Your competitor has abandoned the marketplace.

Competitors' employees make contact with you.
They are worried.

Competitors' employees expose internal problems.
They do not take their companies' management seriously.

A competitor suddenly changes its message and image.
The company is falling apart.

A competitor's top managers are easily angered.
They are stretched too thin.

A competitor starts selling off assets.
The company is short of resources.

A competitor stops paying its bills and closes down offices.
The management has no choice.

A competitor's allies seem to be cooperating.
Nevertheless, they are slow to communicate.
Their alliances are failing.

A competitor offers too many incentives to buy.
That company is not making its sales goals.

ADVANTAGE:

In market competition, you need to take advantage of the problems that your competitors are having.

[39]Your enemy gives out too many punishments.
His men are weary.

[41]Your enemy first acts violently and then is afraid of your
larger force.
His best troops have not arrived.

[43]Your enemy comes in a conciliatory manner.
He needs to rest and recuperate.

[45]Your enemy is angry and appears to welcome battle.
This goes on for a long time, but he doesn't attack.
He also doesn't leave the field.
You must watch him carefully.

If you are too weak to compete, you find more men. 6
In this situation, you must not act aggressively.
You must unite your forces.
Prepare for the enemy.
Recruit men and stay where you are.

[6]You must be cautious about making plans and
adjust to the enemy.
You must gather more men.

EXPANSION:

*Campaigns
into new areas
expand your
control but they
also spread your
resources over a
wider territory.*

Competitors make it more difficult to buy from them.
They have too many bad customers.

A competitor challenges you and then quickly withdraws from your market.
The company needs to develop more resources.

A competitor suggests partnering with you.
That organization is simply buying time.

A competitor sounds aggressive and seems to want your customers.
The company remains in the market without challenging you.
It does not withdraw from the market either.
You must keep your eye on that company.

6 When stretched to the limit, you must hire more people.
At that time, you must not try to challenge competitors.
You must organize your operations.
You must train your people to meet the competition.
You must build up and be patient.

You must do as little as possible while adjusting to
your competitors' movements.
You must increase the size of your organization.

A marketing campaign reaches its limit when your resources are stretched too thin to make more sales.

With new, undedicated soldiers, you can depend on them 7
if you discipline them.
They will tend to disobey your orders.
If they do not obey your orders, they will be useless.

4You can depend on seasoned, dedicated soldiers.
But you must avoid disciplining them without reason.
Otherwise, you cannot use them.

7You must control your soldiers with esprit de corps.
You must bring them together by winning victories.
You must get them to believe in you.

10Make it easy for people to know what to do by training
your people.
Your people will then obey you.
If you do not make it easy for people to know what
to do, you won't train your people.
Then they will not obey.

14Make your commands easy to follow.
You must understand the way a crowd thinks.

✦ ✦ ✦

YOUR TROOPS:

*Your success
depends totally
on your ability to
train, motivate,
and manage
the people with
whom you work.*

7 You can depend on new, untrained employees if you tell them exactly what to do.

Otherwise, they will get confused.

If they are confused, they cannot be productive.

It is different with experienced, proven employees.

You must let them see for themselves what needs to be done.

If you micromanage them, they will go elsewhere.

You must lead your employees by inspiring them.

You unite them by making them successful.

They will believe in you if your predictions come true.

Make it easy for employees to follow directions by making your goals and procedures clear.

They will then do what they must.

If procedures are difficult to understand, you will not be able to train your employees.

They will make too many mistakes.

Make your policies easy to understand.

You must understand how groups of people work.

♦ ♦ ♦

EMPLOYEES:

Entrepreneurs must train and manage the best employees if they wish to master the competition.

Chapter 10

Field Position: Evaluating Opportunities

You have to make choices about what ventures to get involved in. Each opportunity is a stepping-stone to the next. Before you move to a new position, you must judge whether or not it will allow you to move forward more easily in the future. Six characteristics, called field positions, are used to evaluate your opportunities for their future potential. These six characteristics tell you how easily you can defend your new position and use it for future progress.

The six types of field positions—unobstructed, entangling, supporting, constricted, barricaded, and spread out—are all extremes. They represent the extreme points in a three dimensional matrix of dangers, distance, and obstacles. For example, constricted and spread out are the two extremes on the distance axis of this array. In real life, most opportunities are a combination of these factors, where conditions are somewhere between the two extremes.

The six flaws in organizations are amplified by the six extreme forms of field position. You need to recognize and diagnose these weaknesses to predict how a given organization will respond to a certain type of opportunity.

You must consider these issues and more in moving from one temporary position to another. As an entrepreneur, you must provide the right leadership as you move into new situations. Finally, you must compare your relative field position with that of your opponent before choosing any course of action.

Field Position

SUN TZU SAID:

Some field positions are unobstructed. 1
Some field positions are entangling.
Some field positions are supporting.
Some field positions are constricted.
Some field positions give you a barricade.
Some field positions are spread out.

7You can attack from some positions easily.
Other forces can meet you easily as well.
We call these unobstructed positions.
These positions are open.
On them, be the first to occupy a high, sunny area.
Put yourself where you can defend your supply routes.
Then you will have an advantage.

IN THE FIELD:

Strategy teaches that you can learn the true nature of a territory only once you have entered into it.

Evaluating Opportunities

THE BUSINESS WARRIOR HEARS:

1 Some opportunities are wide open.
Some opportunities are sticky.
Some opportunities are optimal.
Some opportunities are exclusive.
Some opportunities are easy to protect.
Some opportunities are too big.

You can take advantage of some opportunities easily.
Competitors can take advantage of them just as easily.
These are wide open opportunities.
These ventures offer no barriers to entry.
Get into these businesses first and get visibility.
Concentrate on creating defensible income streams.
You will then make money from them.

OPPORTUNITY:

There are six different forms of opportunities and each requires the appropriate approach.

[14]You can attack from some positions easily.
Disaster arises when you try to return to them.
These are entangling positions.
These field positions are one-sided.
Wait until your enemy is unprepared.
You can then attack from these positions and win.
Avoid a well-prepared enemy.
You will try to attack and lose.
Since you can't return, you will meet disaster.
These field positions offer no advantage.

[24]You cannot leave some positions without losing an advantage.
If the enemy leaves this ground, he also loses an advantage.
We call these supporting field positions.
These positions strengthen you.
The enemy may try to entice you away.
Still, hold your position.
You must entice the enemy to leave.
You then strike him as he is leaving.
These field positions offer an advantage.

[33]Some field positions are constricted.
Get to these positions first.
You must fill these areas and await the enemy.
Sometimes, the enemy will reach them first.
If he fills them, do not follow him.
However, if he fails to fill them, you can go after him.

You can move on from some opportunities easily.
You destroy these positions once you leave them.
These are sticky opportunities.
These situations give you one chance.
Wait for the right time to move on from them to new opportunities.
You can then move from sticky situations to better opportunities.
Avoid moving from sticky situations into uncertain opportunities.
You can launch your venture and it could fail.
Since you cannot go back to your old position, you are in trouble.
Sticky opportunities offer no long-term advantage.

You cannot move away from some opportunities without taking a step backward.
They do not lead to any better position.
These are optimal opportunities.
They are the strongest possible positions in that area.
A competitor may try to lure you away from them.
You must hold your position.
If competitors are in a peak position, try to lure them away.
You can then take advantage of their poor decisions.
Do not take optimal opportunities for granted.

Some opportunities are exclusive.
You must establish these positions before competitors do.
You must satisfy the need for the product and await competitors.
Competitors may establish themselves in these positions first.
If they satisfy the market, do not try to copy them.
If they leave unsatisfied needs, you can go copy them.

³⁹Some field positions give you a barricade.
Get to these positions first.
You must occupy their southern, sunny heights in order to await the enemy.
Sometimes the enemy occupies these areas first.
If so, entice him away.
Never go after him.

⁴⁵Some field positions are too spread out.
Your force may seem equal to the enemy.
Still you will lose if you provoke a battle.
If you battle, you will not have any advantage.

⁴⁹These are the six types of field positions.
Each battleground has its own rules.
As a commander, you must know where to go.
You must examine each position closely.

Some armies can be outmaneuvered. 2
Some armies are too lax.
Some armies fall down.
Some armies fall apart.
Some armies are disorganized.
Some armies must retreat.

YOUR FORCES:

The term "forces" means all elements used against the competition, both personnel and resources.

⁷Know all six of these weaknesses.
They create weak timing and disastrous positions.
They all arise from the army's commander.

Some opportunities are easy to protect.
You must establish yourself in these areas before competitors do.
You then must aggressively publicize your position and await competitive attacks.
Sometimes competitors win these opportunities first.
If so, try to get your competitors to abandon them.
Do not go after competitors in these positions.

Some opportunities are too big.
They spread your limited resources too thinly to be competitive.
You are wasting your time on these opportunities.
They are too big for you to defend from a competitive challenge.

Know all six types of opportunities.
Each business situation has its own rules.
You must know the type of business you are in.
You must match your position to the opportunity.

2 Some ventures are misguided.
Some ventures are undisciplined.
Some ventures stumble.
Some ventures self-destruct.
Some venture are confused.
Some ventures must pull back.

Recognize these six weaknesses in enterprises.
They make it hard to take advantage of opportunities.
Management decisions create these flaws.

PREDICTION:

If you know the weakness of an enterprise, you can predict the problems that it is likely to have.

¹⁰One general can command a force equal to the enemy.
Still his enemy outflanks him.
This means that his army can be outmaneuvered.

¹³Another can have strong soldiers but weak officers.
This means that his army is too lax.

¹⁵Another has strong officers but weak soldiers.
This means that his army will fall down.

¹⁷Another has subcommanders that are angry and defiant.
They attack the enemy and make their own battles.
The commander cannot know the battlefield.
This means that his army will fall apart.

²¹Another general is weak and easygoing.
He fails to make his orders clear.
His officers and men lack direction.
This shows in his military formations.
This means that his army is disorganized.

²⁶Another general fails to predict the enemy.
He pits his small forces against larger ones.
His weak forces attack stronger ones.
He fails to pick his openings correctly.
This means that his army must retreat.

COMMAND:

*Only one person
makes the key
decisions in an
organization,
thereby shaping
it and creating
any flaws.*

Some entrepreneurs start with the same resources as competitors.
But their competitors know how to deploy those resources better.
This means that their ventures are misguided.

Some entrepreneurs get good work done but make poor decisions.
This means that their ventures are undisciplined.

Some entrepreneurs make good decisions but are poor at execution.
This means that their ventures will stumble.

Some have business partners that are emotional and headstrong.
These partners want to run their operations independently.
These organizations cannot focus on their missions.
This means that their ventures will self-destruct.

Some entrepreneurs are lazy and sloppy.
They fail to make their instructions clear.
Their decisions and procedures are inconsistent.
This shows in their operations.
This means that their ventures are confused.

Some entrepreneurs fail to consider the competition.
They pit limited resources against superior resources.
They pit weak products against superior ones.
They pick the wrong marketplaces.
This means that their ventures must be abandoned.

COMPETITION:

You must avoid opportunities that pit you against com-petitors who have superior resources.

³¹You must know all about these six weaknesses.
You must understand the philosophies that lead to defeat.
When a general arrives, you can know what he will do.
You must study each general carefully.

You must control your field position. 3
It will always strengthen your army.

³You must predict the enemy to overpower him and win.
You must analyze the obstacles, dangers, and distances.
This is the best way to command.

⁶Understand your field position before you go to battle.
Then you will win.
You can fail to understand your field position and still fight.
Then you will lose.

¹⁰You must provoke battle when you will certainly win.
It doesn't matter what you are ordered.
The government may order you not to battle.
Despite that, you must always battle when you will win.

FORESIGHT:

Once you can quickly diagnose a situation, you know the appropriate response when others leave openings.

¹⁴Sometimes provoking a battle will lead to a loss.
The government may order you to battle.
Despite that, you must avoid battle when you will lose.

You must understand all six of these weaknesses.
You must understand the thinking behind them.
When you face competitors, you must recognize their weaknesses.
Your opportunities come from knowing their weaknesses.

3 You must choose to pursue the right opportunities.
They must always make your competitive position stronger.

You must foresee how to outmaneuver competitors.
Think about barriers, future progress, and separation.
This is the only way to build a business.

Design your enterprise to fit the nature of your opportunities.
This is how you make money.
You can invest without understanding your opportunity.
This will always cost you money.

Challenge competitors when they are at a disadvantage.
Forget your original business plans.
You may not have planned on a certain opportunity.
You must go after business when the opportunity is right.

Know when pursuing an opportunity will be costly.
Your company may desire that market.
Still, you must avoid campaigns that cost you more
than they gain.

FLEXIBILITY:

As you learn more about your opportunities, you must be willing to adapt your plans accordingly.

17You must advance without desiring praise.
You must retreat without fearing shame.
The only correct move is to preserve your troops.
This is how you serve your country.
This is how you reward your nation.

Think of your soldiers as little children. 4
You can make them follow you into a deep river.
Treat them as your beloved children.
You can lead them all to their deaths.

5Some leaders are generous but cannot use their men.
They love their men but cannot command them.
Their men are unruly and disorganized.
These leaders create spoiled children.
Their soldiers are useless.

You may know what your soldiers will do in an attack. 5
You may not know if the enemy is vulnerable to attack.
You will then win only half the time.
You may know that the enemy is vulnerable to attack.
You may not know if your men have the capability of attack-
ing him.
You will still win only half the time.
You may know that the enemy is vulnerable to attack.
You may know that your men are ready to attack.
You may not, however, know how to position yourself in the
field for battle.
You will still win only half the time.

Your ventures must make money, not just win awards.
Get out of any enterprise that doesn't pay off.
The only goal is to increase your profits.
This is how you build your organization.
This is how you ensure your success.

4 Think of your business associates as your family.
They will support you in an uncertain future.
Develop business relationships with care and understanding.
They will serve you faithfully.

Some entrepreneurs invest in relationships but cannot use them.
They like partnerships but do not take a leadership role in them.
This results in confused and unproductive relationships.
You cannot be unclear about partner responsibilities.
Such business relationships are useless.

5 You may know that your enterprise is ready for an opportunity.
You must also know that your competitors will make mistakes.
If you do not, your venture will be successful only half the time.
You may know that your competitors are creating an opportunity.
However, you must also know that your enterprise can take advantage of that type of opportunity.
If you do not, your venture will be successful only half the time.
You can recognize the opportunity in your competitors' mistakes.
You can know your enterprise is ready for an opportunity.
However, you must also know exactly how to make the best use of that specific type of opportunity.
If you do not, your venture will be successful only half the time.

[11]You must know how to make war.
You can then act without confusion.
You can attempt anything.

[14]We say:
Know the enemy and know yourself.
Your victory will be painless.
Know the weather and the field.
Your victory will be complete.

RELATIVITY:

Your qualities, both good and bad, are important only in comparison with your opponents' qualities.

You must know how to be competitive.
Your path is then completely certain.
The sky is the limit.

Strategy dictates:
Know your competitors and your own capabilities.
Then it is safe to invest money.
Understand market trends and your marketplace.
Then your profits are assured.

SYNTHESIS:

*Strategy ac-
knowledges that
you cannot know
everything but
that you must
master a few
key factors.*

Chapter 11

九地

Types of Terrain: Progressing Through Stages

As a new venture or a project moves forward, it passes through nine common situations or stages. Each of these stages poses a specific type of challenge. Each of these challenges requires a specific response. The key to moving forward quickly is instantly recognizing and reacting to these situations as they arise. Inappropriate reactions make each of these situations worse and slow down your progress. Since speed is the essence of war, business warriors train themselves to instantly recognize these situations and to respond by reflex.

In these stages, the earliest steps are usually the easiest and you have the most options. As you make progress, the challenges from competition get more difficult. You have fewer and fewer options until the final stages, which are the most difficult and desperate.

The increasing difficulty of a new venture over time makes sense because each step forward takes you further into new territory. At the beginning, you are relatively close to home and your only challenge is defending against larger opponents. As you move further and further into new territory, more and more complications arise.

Through the entire process, you must maintain the pace of progress. A good leader learns how to use the increasing pressure from competitors to unite and focus the enterprise. The psychological pressures of business can destroy an organization if a leader doesn't immediately know how to respond.

Types of Terrain

GROUND:

Ground, territory, and terrain are all from the same Chinese concept, "di," which also means situation and condition.

SUN TZU SAID:

Use the art of war. 1
Know when the terrain will scatter you.
Know when the terrain will be easy.
Know when the terrain will be disputed.
Know when the terrain is open.
Know when the terrain is intersecting.
Know when the terrain is dangerous.
Know when the terrain is bad.
Know when the terrain is confined.
Know when the terrain is deadly.

¹¹Warring parties must sometimes battle inside
their own territory.
This is scattering terrain.

¹³When you enter hostile territory, your penetration
is shallow.
This is easy terrain.

¹⁵Some terrain gives you an advantageous position.
But it gives others an advantageous position as well.
This will be disputed terrain.

Progressing Through Stages

THE BUSINESS WARRIOR HEARS:

1 Use your strategic skills.
Know when a situation is dissipating.
Know when a situation is easy.
Know when a situation is contentious.
Know when a situation is open.
Know when a situation is shared.
Know when a situation is serious.
Know when a situation is difficult.
Know when a situation is limited.
Know when a situation is desperate.

STAGES:

The nine stages described here explain a logical evolution that ventures go through as they continue.

You must sometimes defend against competitors coming into your market.
This is the dissipating stage.

When you move into a new market, your product is a novelty.
This is the easy stage.

Some markets generate profitable business for you.
Nevertheless, competitors can win these profitable sales as well.
This is the contentious stage.

18You can use some terrain to advance easily.
Others can advance along with you.
This is open terrain.

21Everyone shares access to a given area.
The first one to arrive there can gather a larger group than
anyone else.
This is intersecting terrain.

24You can penetrate deeply into hostile territory.
Then many hostile cities are behind you.
This is dangerous terrain.

27There are mountain forests.
There are dangerous obstructions.
There are reservoirs.
Everyone confronts these obstacles on a campaign.
They make bad terrain.

32In some areas, the entry passage is narrow.
You are closed in as you try to get out of them.
In this type of area, a few people can effectively attack your
much larger force.
This is confined terrain.

36You can sometimes survive only if you battle quickly.
You will die if you delay.
This is deadly terrain.

You make easy progress building your enterprise.
Competitors, however, are also building their businesses.
This is the open stage.

Several noncompeting companies also sell to your market.
If you can develop good partnerships with them, you will dominate the market.
This is the shared stage.

You invest heavily to build your market position.
Competitors still have many devoted allies in the market.
This is the serious stage.

You run into problems that slow the venture down.
You encounter barriers to winning the market.
Unforeseen changes take place.
These obstacles are unavoidable in making progress.
This is the difficult stage.

In some ventures, there is a key transition point.
Your options are severely limited.
Your entire business is an easy target if competitors know what your limited options are.
This is the limited stage.

You can win only if you commit all your resources.
You will lose your business if you delay.
This is the desperate stage.

[39]To be successful, you must control scattering terrain by avoiding battle.

Control easy terrain by not stopping.

Control disputed terrain by not attacking.

Control open terrain by staying with the enemy's forces.

Control intersecting terrain by uniting with your allies.

Control dangerous terrain by plundering.

Control bad terrain by keeping on the move.

Control confined terrain by using surprise.

Control deadly terrain by battling.

Go to an area that is known to be good for waging war. 2
Use it to cut off the enemy's contact between his front and back lines.

Prevent his small parties from relying on his larger force.

Stop his strong divisions from rescuing his weak ones.

Prevent his officers from getting their men together.

Chase his soldiers apart to stop them from amassing.

Harass them to prevent their ranks from forming.

[8]When joining battle gives you an advantage, you must do it.

When it isn't to your benefit, you must avoid it.

CONTROL:

Each of the nine "terrains," "conditions," or "stages" demands a specific form of response.

[10]A daring soldier may ask:

"A large, organized enemy army and its general are coming.

What do I do to prepare for them?"

To be successful, you avoid the dissipating stage by distracting the competition.

During the easy stage, you must keep moving.

During the contentious stage, you avoid tempting new markets.

In the open stage, you keep up with competitors.

In the shared stage, you make partnerships.

In the serious stage, you concentrate on generating income.

In the difficult stage, you press forward.

In the limited stage, you must do the unexpected.

In the desperate stage, you use everything you have.

2 You want to meet competitors in their markets, not yours.

You need to distract larger competitors moving into your markets by forcing them to defend their markets.

You can always target a segment of their market to harass them.

Target areas in which your competitors are weakest.

Mislead their managers about the value of your target market.

Undermine test marketing to discourage more investment.

Make sure all of their early attempts are stopped before they start.

When you have an obvious advantage, force comparisons.

When you do not have an advantage, avoid comparisons.

DIVISION:

You wonder:

"A big, organized competitor is clearly moving into my market.

What should I do?"

When defending against specific competitors, you must try to divide their focus, resources, and positions.

¹³Tell him:

"First seize an area that the enemy must have.

Then he will pay attention to you.

Mastering speed is the essence of war.

Take advantage of a large enemy's inability to keep up.

Use a philosophy of avoiding difficult situations.

Attack the area where he doesn't expect you."

You must use the philosophy of an invader. 3

Invade deeply and then concentrate your forces.

This controls your men without oppressing them.

⁴Get your supplies from the riches of the territory.

It is sufficient to supply your whole army.

⁶Take care of your men and do not overtax them.

Your esprit de corps increases your momentum.

Keep your army moving and plan for surprises.

Make it difficult for the enemy to count your forces.

Position your men where there is no place to run.

They will then face death without fleeing.

They will find a way to survive.

Your officers and men will use every ounce of effort.

¹⁴Military officers who are committed lose their fear.

When they have nowhere to run, they must stand firm.

Deep in enemy territory, they are captives.

Since they cannot escape, they will fight.

There is an answer.
First, move into key markets of theirs before they move into yours.
Then your competitors must pay attention to their markets.
A small enterprise can move more quickly than a large one.
You can move from customer to customer faster than they can.
You don't want to actually battle them for their business.
You want them to focus on defending their own territory.

3 As an entrepreneur, you must move into new areas.
Your commitment to new ventures gives you focus.
This focus unites your enterprise without limiting it.

You must generate profits quickly from new markets.
Profits by themselves can pay for your venture's growth.

Take care of your employees and do not overburden them.
Share your company's success with your people.
Keep your employees busy and keep their jobs interesting.
Make it difficult for competitors to steal your people.
Create an enterprise that holds experienced employees.
They will then defend the enterprise without abandoning it.
People find solutions to challenges.
If people are dedicated, they will work hard for you.

When people are dependent on your business, they lose their fear.
When they have no alternatives, they will stay with you.
If you are committed to your customers, employees will stay.
Since they have nowhere else to go, they will work hard.

[18]Commit your men completely.
Without being posted, they will be on guard.
Without being asked, they will get what is needed.
Without being forced, they will be dedicated.
Without being given orders, they can be trusted.

[23]Stop them from guessing by removing all their doubts.
Stop them from dying by giving them no place to run.

[25]Your officers may not be rich.
Nevertheless, they still desire plunder.
They may die young.
Nevertheless, they still want to live forever.

[29]You must order the time of attack.
Officers and men may sit and weep until their lapels are wet.
When they stand up, tears may stream down their cheeks.
Put them in a position where they cannot run.
They will show the greatest courage under fire.

Make good use of war. 4
This demands instant reflexes.
You must develop these instant reflexes.
Act like an ordinary mountain snake.
If people strike your head then stop them with your tail.
If they strike your tail then stop them with your head.
If they strike your middle then use both your head and tail.

Involve your employees completely.
Without being told, everyone must know what to do.
Without being asked, everyone must see what is needed.
Without being forced, everyone must be dedicated.
Without being instructed, everyone must be trusted.

Stop any second-guessing by making your direction clear.
Avoid failure by leaving your people no excuses.

You and your employees may not be rich.
This is not because you do not want to win wealth.
You may all fail together.
It should not be because you were not committed to success.

You must insist on moving into new areas quickly.
Your employees will complain that they cannot meet the deadlines.
When they must do it, they still will tell you that they cannot.
Put them in a position where they have no choice.
They will find a way to get the work done.

4 You must think competitively.
You need to develop quick reflexes.
You must respond to situations automatically.
You must be able to act on instinct.
If attacked at a venture's beginning, you can win in the end.
If challenged at the end, you can win by starting on the right foot.
If threatened in between, win by starting well and finishing strong.

[8]A daring soldier asks:
"Can any army imitate these instant reflexes?"
We answer:
"It can."

[12]To command and get the most out of proud people, you
must study adversity.
People work together when they are in the same boat
during a storm.
In this situation, one rescues the other just as the
right hand helps the left.

ADVERSITY:

*Strategically,
unity is strength,
and nothing
unites a force
more than being
threatened by a
common enemy.*

[15]Use adversity correctly.
Tether your horses and bury your wagons' wheels.
Still, you can't depend on this alone.
An organized force is braver than lone individuals.
This is the art of organization.
Put the tough and weak together.
You must also use the terrain.

[22]Make good use of war.
Unite your men as one.
Never let them give up.

The commander must be a military professional. 5
This requires confidence and detachment.
You must maintain dignity and order.
You must control what your men see and hear.
They must follow you without knowing your plans.

You may question these reflexes.

Should your business respond instantly to attack?

There is only one answer.

It must!

To lead and control people, you must understand the uniting power of opposition.

People come together when they share the same threats and challenges.

When people are bound together by mutual self-interest, they automatically come to each other's aid.

Use the opposition correctly.

Make it hard for your people to abandon you.

Even this is not enough.

A team is more courageous than any individual.

This is the art of teamwork.

Team your best and worst employees together.

Make them respond appropriately to the situation.

LEADERSHIP:

People readily follow courageous leaders with a clear vision who create a sense of shared mission.

Make good use of competition.

Unite the people in your enterprise.

Lead them through every stage.

5 An entrepreneur must be a professional.

This requires confidence and detachment.

You must maintain your leadership and focus.

You must control what your employees see and hear.

They must believe in you without your explaining your reasoning.

[6]You can reinvent your men's roles.

You can change your plans.

You can use your men without their understanding.

[9]You must shift your campgrounds.

You must take detours from the ordinary routes.

You must use your men without giving them your strategy.

[12]A commander provides what is needed now.

This is like climbing high and being willing to kick away your ladder.

You must be able to lead your men deeply into different surrounding territory.

And yet, you can discover the opportunity to win.

[16]You must drive men like a flock of sheep.

You must drive them to march.

You must drive them to attack.

You must never let them know where you are headed.

You must unite them into a great army.

You must then drive them against all opposition.

This is the job of a true commander.

[23]You must adapt to the different terrain.

You must adapt to find an advantage.

You must manage your people's affections.

You must study all these skills.

You can reinvent people's jobs.

You can change your direction.

You must lead people without having to defend your decisions.

You must be able to change your location.

You must be able to change your business procedures.

Your people must accept changes without your explaining everything.

You must provide exactly what the enterprise needs at the moment.

You must be willing to go out on a limb and take a risk in your investment.

You must get your people deeply involved in new markets related to your existing business.

This is how they discover opportunities for success.

You must lead your people because they need a leader.

You must inspire them to act.

You must force them into new areas.

You must not let them take the current direction for granted.

You must organize them into a powerful enterprise.

You must set them totally against your competitors.

This is the work of a true entrepreneur.

You must respond appropriately to your stage of progress.

You must take advantage of new openings.

You must control your people's emotions.

You must master the principles of strategy.

Always use the philosophy of invasion. 6

Deep invasions concentrate your forces.

Shallow invasions scatter your forces.

When you leave your country and cross the border, you must take control.

This is always critical ground.

You can sometimes move in any direction.

This is always intersecting ground.

You can penetrate deeply into a territory.

This is always dangerous ground.

You penetrate only a little way.

This is always easy ground.

Your retreat is closed and the path ahead tight.

This is always confined ground.

There is sometimes no place to run.

This is always deadly ground.

[16]To use scattering terrain correctly, you must inspire your men's devotion.

On easy terrain, you must keep in close communication.

On disputed terrain, you must hamper the enemy's progress.

On open terrain, you must carefully defend your chosen position.

On intersecting terrain, you must solidify your alliances.

On dangerous terrain, you must ensure your food supplies.

On bad terrain, you must keep advancing along the road.

On confined terrain, you must stop information leaks from your headquarters.

On deadly terrain, you must show what you can do by killing the enemy.

6 Your mission must be to move into new areas.
Serious commitment focuses your efforts.
Lack of commitment dissipates your resources.
When you leave what you know and first start a new venture, you must take the lead.
This is a critical stage.
You and other businesspeople can have common interests.
This is the shared stage.
You can invest all your reserves in a new venture.
This is always the serious stage.
All ventures look promising when you first get into them.
This is always the easy stage of making progress.
You cannot back out and you have too few options in the future.
This is the limited stage of progress.
An enterprise's future can depend on the resolution of a crisis.
This is the desperate stage.

To succeed in the dissipating stage, you must have your customers' commitment.
In the easy stage, you must communicate with customers.
In the contentious stage, you must create obstacles for competitors.
In the open stage, you must win your own group of customers.
In the shared stage, you must join your partners.
In the serious stage, you must generate income.
In the difficult stage, you must keep your venture moving.
In the limited stage, you must not let your competitors know you are vulnerable.
In the desperate stage, you must prove yourself by putting an end to the crisis.

²⁵Make your men feel like an army.
Surround them and they will defend themselves.
If they cannot avoid it, they will fight.
If they are under pressure, they will obey.

Do the right thing when you don't know your 7
different enemies' plans.
Don't attempt to meet them.

³You don't know the position of mountain forests, dangerous
obstructions, and reservoirs?
Then you cannot march the army.
You don't have local guides?
You won't get any of the benefits of the terrain.

⁷There are many factors in war.
You may lack knowledge of any one of them.
If so, it is wrong to take a nation into war.

¹⁰You must be able to control your management of war.
If you divide a big nation, it will be unable to put together a
large force.
Increase your enemy's fear of your ability.
Prevent his forces from getting together and
organizing.

KNOWLEDGE:

Strategy teaches that you can replace investment of time and effort with more complete information.

Make your people feel like they are winners.
Make them face the challenge and they will succeed.
When they have no choice, they will give it all they have.
When people are committed, they will follow your lead.

7 Make the safe decisions when you have not analyzed your competitors' positions.
Do not try to compete with them.

You do not know the types of barriers, dangers, and distances in a new area?
Then you cannot venture into it.
You don't have information on a market's customers?
Then you will not see opportunities in that market.

There is so much to know to compete in business.
You cannot cut yourself off from any category of news.
Without information, you cannot make progress.

You must organize your direction in competition.
To dissect large competitors, you isolate small segments of their business.
You make them nervous about your success.
This stops them from getting together more resources to invest.

REEVALUATE:

Analysis must be repeated constantly as you reexamine the five key factors that define your position.

¹⁴Do the right thing and do not arrange outside alliances
before their time.
You will not have to assert your authority prematurely.
Trust only yourself and your self-interest.
This increases the enemy's fear of you.
You can make one of his allies withdraw.
His whole nation can fall.

²⁰Distribute rewards without worrying about having a system.
Halt without the government's command.
Attack with the whole strength of your army.
Use your army as if it were a single man.

²⁴Attack with skill.
Do not discuss it.
Attack when you have an advantage.
Do not talk about the dangers.
When you can launch your army into deadly ground, even if
it stumbles, it can still survive.
You can be weakened in a deadly battle and yet be stronger
afterward.

³⁰Even a large force can fall into misfortune.
If you fall behind, however, you can still turn defeat into victory.
You must use the skills of war.
To survive, you must adapt yourself to your enemy's purpose.
You must stay with him no matter where he goes.
It may take a thousand miles to kill the general.
If you correctly understand him, you can find the skill to do it.

You make the best progress if you put off partnerships as long as possible.

Then you will not have to fight for leadership.

Trust your decisions and your own resources.

This decreases your competitors' sources of intelligence.

You may convince your competitors' allies to abandon them.

Their whole business can then fail.

Reward those who work with you according to their merit.

You don't compete to satisfy your internal operations.

Commit to proven new areas with all your resources.

Focus your resources totally on the goal at hand.

Make strategic progress.

Do not explain your mission.

Move immediately when you see an opening.

Do not let others know your weaknesses.

You can move through desperate stages where mistakes are made and still make progress.

You can be drained in desperate struggles and still find the fulfillment of progress.

A solid enterprise can have the climate turn against it.

If you make errors, you can still turn initial failure into ultimate success.

You must use the science of strategy.

Your venture must respond to your competitors' missions.

You must keep up with your competitors no matter what.

You may have to go a long way before finding their fatal flaws.

If you understand competitive thinking, you can find a way to win.

Manage your government correctly at the start of a war. 8
Close your borders and tear up passports.
Block the passage of envoys.
Encourage politicians at headquarters to stay out of it.
You must use any means to put an end to politics.
Your enemy's people will leave you an opening.
You must instantly invade through it.

[8]Immediately seize a place that they love.
Do it quickly.
Trample any border to pursue the enemy.
Use your judgment about when to battle.

[12]Doing the right thing at the start of war is like approaching a woman.
Your enemy's men must open the door.
After that, you should act like a streaking rabbit.
The enemy will be unable to catch you.

✦ ✦ ✦

BEGINNINGS:

The start of a campaign is a delicate time when you set the direction for the entire course of the campaign.

8 Make good decisions when you target a competitive market.
Protect your existing customers and keep competitors out.
Put up a blanket of secrecy.
Do not let your internal operations make the decisions.
Eliminate anything that disturbs your competitive focus.
Your competitors will create an opportunity for you.
Quickly move into markets they leave open.

Quickly win the most profitable customers.
Waste no time.
Eliminate barriers that protect your competition.
Make good decisions about where to compete.

Success in the early stages of progress comes from wooing your customers.
Your competitors will eventually neglect their business.
When they do, you should act quickly.
Never let your competitors catch up with you.

✦ ✦ ✦

OPENINGS:

You cannot win markets without the cooperation of competitors who leave you the openings that you need.

Chapter 12

Attacking With Fire: Reinventing an Industry

Competing within an industry is an acceptable strategy, but reinventing an industry is much better. Entrepreneurs must master creative destruction. This chapter of *The Art of War* explains the use of a specific weapon—fire—but its broader application is using the environment as a weapon to destroy existing ways of doing business. Harness the destructive power of the environment and you can eliminate your competition.

Creative destruction is addition by subtraction. You eliminate what is unnecessary to increase the value of what is left. Technological change transforms activities and resources that were once necessary into waste. You start this process by picking a target. All enemies, including waste, offer five potential targets.

Changes in the business climate make these attacks possible. Timing is critical in finding an opportunity for these attacks. You cannot destroy an old model until people are ready for a new one. The attack itself is less important than the response to it. The attack itself does not create the opportunity. It is the response by customers, employees, and competitors that creates the opportunity.

Creative change, symbolized by water, is also an environmental weapon, but the use of destructive change, symbolized by fire, has advantages that creative change cannot match. All change is emotional. Change creates the fear of the unknown. Destructive change is especially frightening. You need to control your emotional responses in both undertaking and responding to these attacks.

Attacking With Fire

FIRE:

FIRE:

Classical strategy describes the element of fire as a weapon and uses it as a metaphor for all weapons.

SUN TZU SAID:

There are five ways of attacking with fire. 1
The first is burning troops.
The second is burning supplies.
The third is burning supply transport.
The fourth is burning storehouses.
The fifth is burning camps.

⁷To make fire, you must have the resources.
To build a fire, you must prepare the raw materials.

⁹To attack with fire, you must be in the right season.
To start a fire, you must have the time.

¹¹Choose the right season.
The weather must be dry.

¹³Choose the right time.
Pick a season when the grass is as high as the side of a cart.

¹⁵You can tell the proper days by the stars in the night sky.
You want days when the wind rises in the morning.

Reinventing an Industry

THE BUSINESS WARRIOR HEARS:

1 There are five ways to reinvent an industry.
First, you can eliminate people.
Second, you can eliminate time.
Third, you can eliminate transportation.
Fourth, you can eliminate inventory.
Fifth, you can eliminate locations.

DESTRUCTION:

You recreate an industry by destroying the elements that are unnecessary for the existing industry.

To destroy an old business model, you need an opportunity.
To create a change, you need a new approach.

To destroy an existing industry, the business climate must be right.
To ignite a change, you invest time in the new process.

Choose the right year.
A tight business climate requires lower-cost alternatives.

Choose the right time.
The technological fuel must be readily available.

You can know when to ignite change by studying the signs.
You want a time when people are ready for a new beginning.

Everyone attacks with fire. 2
You must create five different situations with fire and be able
to adjust to them.

3You start a fire inside the enemy's camp.
Then attack the enemy's periphery.

5You launch a fire attack, but the enemy remains calm.
Wait and do not attack.

7The fire reaches its height.
Follow its path if you can.
If you can't follow it, stay where you are.

REACTION:

The environment is unpredictable so you must always act based upon how situations develop rather than on your plans.

10Spreading fires on the outside of camp can kill.
You can't always get fire inside the enemy's camp.
Take your time in spreading it.

13Set the fire when the wind is at your back.
Don't attack into the wind.
Daytime winds last a long time.
Night winds fade quickly.

17Every army must know how to adjust to the five
possible attacks by fire.
Use many men to guard against them.

2 Everyone tries to eliminate waste.
You must prepare for five different types of industry changes and
adapt them to move into new areas.

You can eliminate features central to competitors' products.
Then target their marginal customers who don't need those features.

When you reinvent a process, competitors ignore you.
Prove the methods before going into their marketplace.

The renovation of a process can become a fad.
You must follow up on the market's interest right away.
If you cannot move quickly, hold your position.

Small changes outside an industry can destroy it.
You cannot always attack an industry directly.
These changes take time to spread.

Destroy old methods when the trends support you.
Do not fight trends in technology or thinking.
Highly visible trends last a long time.
Less visible trends fade quickly.

CONTROL:

*The less control
you have over
the way others
react, the more
control you must
have over the
way you react.*

You must master these five rules for creative destruction in reinventing an industry.
You must also protect all your ventures against them.

When you use fire to assist your attacks, you are clever. 3
Water can add force to an attack.
You can also use water to disrupt an enemy.
It does not, however, take his resources.

You win in battle by getting the opportunity to attack. 4
It is dangerous if you fail to study how to accomplish this
achievement.
As commander, you cannot waste your opportunities.

[4]We say:
A wise leader plans success.
A good general studies it.
If there is little to be gained, don't act.
If there is little to win, do not use your men.
If there is no danger, do not battle.

[10]As leader, you cannot let your anger interfere with the success of your forces.
As commander, you cannot let yourself become
enraged before you go to battle.
Join the battle only when it is in your advantage
to act.
If there is no advantage in joining a battle, stay
put.

DECISIONS:

Your decisions must use the emotion of others. Your emotions cannot determine your decisions.

3 Creative destruction is the wisest form of competition.
Any innovation can help you win new territory.
Any innovation can put competitors on the defensive.
Creative destruction, however, eliminates their assets.

4 You beat the competition by finding openings to expand.
It is a mistake if you don't look for opportunities to reinvent your industry.
In running a new venture, you cannot waste any opening.

Strategy dictates:
You must know how to build a position.
You must analyze how to make that position competitive.
If an action doesn't make you money, do not take it.
If it cannot be profitable, do not waste your efforts.
If your enterprise is safe, do not risk your resources.

You must never let your emotions affect the success of your enterprise.
As an entrepreneur, you must not make changes simply to create problems for competitors.
Make problems for competitors only when it creates an opening for you.
If there is no profit in reinventing your industry, avoid doing it.

SUCCESS:

A great innovative idea is not one that wins great recognition. It is one that makes a great profit.

¹⁴Anger can change back into happiness.

Rage can change back into joy.

A nation once destroyed cannot be brought back to life.

Dead men do not return to the living.

¹⁸This fact must make a wise leader cautious.

A good general is on guard.

²⁰Your philosophy must be to keep the nation peaceful and the army intact.

EMOTION:

*Emotional grati-
fication is never
the goal of a
competition. You
must never lose
sight of your
goals in the heat
of battle.*

Situations that upset you now may one day make you happy.
Frustration can lead to pleasure.
If you change an industry, you cannot change it back.
What you lose in the process is lost forever.

Knowing this, you must be careful.
A good entrepreneur protects the enterprise.

Your mission must be to keep the enterprise together and keep your ventures competitive.

THE PAYOFF:

Change is not a goal, but only the means to an end. Destruction only makes sense if it creates a stronger position.

Chapter 13

Using Spies: Gathering Information

The application of strategy is a recursive process. Each time you advance your position, you start again at the beginning of the progress cycle by listening. This final chapter emphasizes this by returning us to the starting point for strategic analysis: gathering information. Though we traditionally translate this idea in terms of spies, the original Chinese term actually means "go-between" or "conduit" of information.

The many costs of competition can be minimized by the right information. The entire science of strategy is built around the idea that you use information to replace the more costly assets of time, effort, and physical resources. Good information guides you toward the right things to do as well as teaching you how to do things right.

This information must come from people because strategy is built on leveraging psychology, and only people can tell you what they are thinking. There are five different types of information that you need. They are based on the five key factors introduced in the first chapter. Here we revisit those key factors in identifying the needed information sources.

Gathering information is not a passive process. It requires constant evaluation and people management skills. Before you tackle a specific problem, you must first have sources that provide a complete picture of that problem. The history of competition shows that the most successful entrepreneurs are those who are the most skillful at cultivating good information sources.

Using Spies

SUN TZU SAID:

All successful armies require thousands of men. 1
They invade and march thousands of miles.
Whole families are destroyed.
Other families must be heavily taxed.
Every day, a large amount of money must be spent.

6Internal and external events force people to move.
They are unable to work while on the road.
They are unable to find and hold a useful job.
This affects 70 percent of thousands of families.

10You can watch and guard for years.
Then a single battle can determine victory in a day.
Despite this, bureaucrats worship the value of
their salary money too dearly.
They remain ignorant of the enemy's condition.
The result is cruel.

15They are not leaders of men.
They are not servants of the state.
They are not masters of victory.

ECONOMICS:

*The science of
strategy is based
on the idea that
better informa-
tion can be used
to eliminate
other costs.*

Gathering Information

The business warrior hears:

1 A successful enterprise affects thousands of people.
As an entrepreneur, you labor and work thousands of hours.
Failure threatens your family.
You can invest your whole life's savings.
Every day, your venture consumes your limited resources.

Internal and external events force business ventures to shut down.
It is costly moving from one business to another.
Most of your ventures can fail to make money.
Eighty percent of new ventures fail within two years.

You can run an enterprise for years.
Then a single opportunity can determine its success.
Despite this, many entrepreneurs invest their money
in labor and inventory.
They don't invest in information.
The result is devastating.

Without information, you cannot run an enterprise.
You cannot create value for customers.
You cannot be successful.

Intelligence:

Industries are always dominated by the competitors that have the best information about customers.

[18]You need a creative leader and a worthy commander.
You must move your troops to the right places to beat others.
You must accomplish your attack and escape unharmed.
This requires foreknowledge.
You can obtain foreknowledge.
You can't get it from demons or spirits.
You can't see it from professional experience.
You can't check it with analysis.
You can only get it from other people.
You must always know the enemy's situation.

You must use five types of spies. 2
You need local spies.
You need inside spies.
You need double agents.
You need doomed spies.
You need surviving spies.

[7]You need all five types of spies.
No one must discover your methods.
You will then be able to put together a true picture.
This is the commander's most valuable resource.

NETWORKS:

The key to gathering useful information is to have a range of different types of sources in your network.

[11]You need local spies.
Get them by hiring people from the countryside.

[13]You need inside spies.
Win them by subverting government officials.

You must be innovative and productive.

You must put your resources in the right places.

You must expand in a competitive environment.

This requires advanced information.

You can gather this information.

You will not get it from business theory.

You will not get it from past experience.

You cannot reason it out.

You can only get it by listening to other people.

You must always know your competitive situation.

2 You need to manage five types of information.

You need to know people in your industry.

You need to know your customers.

You need to know your competitors.

You need to create a market image.

You need to know the sales trends.

You must use all five types of information.

You need to gather information that others do not have.

You need a well-rounded perspective on your situation.

Your unique viewpoint gives you a unique insight.

INDIVIDUALS:

You need information on your industry.

Obtain it by developing contacts through the industry.

You need to build personal relationships to get the intelligence that makes a competitive difference.

You need information on your customers.

Ask them what they have on their minds.

¹⁵You need double agents.
Discover enemy agents and convert them.

¹⁷You need doomed spies.
Deceive professionals into being captured.
Let them know your orders.
They then take those orders to your enemy.

²¹You need surviving spies.
Someone must return with a report.

Your job is to build a complete army. 3
No relations are as intimate as the ones with spies.
No rewards are too generous for spies.
No work is as secret as that of spies.

⁵If you aren't clever and wise, you can't use spies.
If you aren't fair and just, you can't use spies.
If you can't see the small subtleties, you won't get the truth
from spies.

⁸Pay attention to small, trifling details!
Spies are helpful in every area.

¹⁰Spies are the first to hear information, so they must not
spread information.
Spies who give your location or talk to others must be killed
along with those to whom they have talked.

You need information on your competition.
You want to win over those who are working with them.

You need to create a market image.
You can control the perceptions of the trade media and analysts.
Let them know what you want others to know.
You should expect them to tell your competitors.

You need recent sales information.
You must analyze which of your sales are making the most money.

3 Your job is to build a complete enterprise.
No resources are as critical as information sources.
No reward is too generous for key information.
Nothing is as sensitive as confidential information.

You must be smart enough to put together the pieces.
You must be open and unbiased to evaluate what you hear.
If you aren't sensitive to subtleties, you will not develop a valuable perspective.

You must pay close attention to small details.
Contacts are helpful in every area.

Your contacts must gather information for your business, but they must not spread it.
Contacts who discuss your strategic positioning with competitors must be cut off.

You may want to attack an army's position. 4
You may want to attack a certain fortification.
You may want to kill people in a certain place.
You must first know the guarding general.
You must know his left and right flanks.
You must know his hierarchy.
You must know the way in.
You must know where different people are stationed.
You must demand this information from your spies.

[10]You want to know the enemy spies in order to convert
them into your men.
You find a source of information and bribe them.
You must bring them in with you.
You must obtain them as double agents and use them as
your emissaries.

[14]Do this correctly and carefully.
You can contact both local and inside spies and obtain their
support.
Do this correctly and carefully.

SPECIFICS:

*The more spe-
cific your targets
become, the
more specific
the information
needed to win
them.*

You create doomed spies by deceiving profession-
als.
You can use them to give false information.
Do this correctly and carefully.
You must have surviving spies capable of bringing
you information at the right time.

4 You may want to target a specific new market.

You may want to take the lead in a certain product category.

You may want to take over a certain geographical territory.

You must first know who your competition's decision-makers are.

You must know how they are defending their position.

You must understand how they are organized.

You must find an opening in the market.

You must discover where the key customers and suppliers are.

You must get this information directly from your contacts.

You want to know where your competitors get their information so you can win their contacts over.

You must be willing to pay the price for information.

You must share information of value with them.

You must develop contacts who know your competitors and treat these contacts as your missionaries within a market.

You must do this carefully and avoid making mistakes.

You can hire from within the industry and your competitors to win competitive knowledge.

You must also do this selectively.

You create an image by controlling the perceptions of the trade media.

You get analysts interested by enticing them.

You must do this carefully as well.

You need detailed information on what you are selling successfully at all times.

INSIDERS:

Your goal is to get inside the information loop used by your customers and competitors.

²¹These are the five different types of intelligence work.
You must be certain to master them all.
You must be certain to create double agents.
You cannot afford to be too cost conscious in creating these double agents.

This technique created the success of ancient Shang. 5
This is how the Shang held its dynasty.

³You must always be careful of your success.
Learn from Lu Ya of Shang.

⁵Be a smart commander and a good general.
You do this by using your best and brightest people for spying.
This is how you achieve the greatest success.
This is how you meet the necessities of war.
The whole army's position and ability to move depends on these spies.

SOURCES:

Strategy is the science of leveraging information sources.

There are five different types of contacts.
You must be certain to use them all.
You must get information from inside your competition.
It is impossible to invest too much time in understanding what your competitors are doing.

5 This is how entrepreneurs create successful ventures.
This is how they have beaten their competitors.

You must always take care of your success.
Study the history of business.

You must be an informed and capable competitive leader.
You get the best information from the smartest people.
This information is the basis for your success.
This is how you survive the challenges of competition.
Your enterprise's current position and future advances depend on good information sources.

SUCCESS:

Success is based only on access to superior knowledge.

Glossary of Key Strategic Concepts

This glossary is keyed to the most common English words used in the translation of *The Art of War*. Those terms only capture the strategic concepts generally. Though translated as English nouns, verbs, adverbs, or adjectives, the Chinese characters on which they are based are totally conceptual, not parts of speech. For example, the character for CONFLICT is translated as the noun "conflict," as the verb "fight," and as the adjective "disputed." Ancient written Chinese was a conceptual language, not a spoken one. More like mathematical terms, these concepts are primarily defined by the strict structure of their relationships with other concepts. The Chinese names shown in parentheses with the characters are primarily based on Pinyin, but we occasionally use Cantonese terms to make each term unique.

ADVANCE (JEUN 進): to move into new GROUND; to expand your POSITION; to move forward in a campaign; the opposite of FLEE.

ADVANTAGE, *benefit* (LI 利): an opportunity arising from having a better POSITION relative to an ENEMY; an opening left by an ENEMY; a STRENGTH that matches against an ENEMY'S WEAKNESS; where fullness meets emptiness; a desirable characteristic of a strategic POSITION.

AIM, *vision, foresee* (JIAN 見): FOCUS on a specific ADVANTAGE, opening, or opportunity; predicting movements of an ENEMY; a skill of a LEADER in observing CLIMATE.

ANALYSIS, *plan* (GAI 計): a comparison of relative POSITION; the examination of the five factors that define a strategic POSITION; a combination of KNOWLEDGE and VISION; the ability to see through DECEPTION.

ARMY: see WAR.

ATTACK, *invade* (GONG 攻): a movement to new GROUND; advancing a strategic POSITION; action against an ENEMY in the sense of moving into his GROUND; opposite of DEFEND; does not necessarily mean CONFLICT.

BAD, *ruined* (PI 圯): a condition of the GROUND that makes ADVANCE difficult; destroyed; terrain that is broken and difficult to traverse; one of the nine situations or types of terrain.

BARRICADED: see OBSTACLES.

BATTLE (ZHAN 戰): to challenge; to engage an ENEMY; generically, to meet a challenge; to choose a confrontation with an ENEMY at a specific time and place; to focus all your resources on a task; to establish superiority in a POSITION; to challenge an ENEMY to increase CHAOS; that which is CONTROLLED by SURPRISE; one of the four forms of ATTACK; the response to a DESPERATE SITUATION; character meaning was originally "big meeting," though later took on the meaning "big weapon"; not necessarily CONFLICT.

BRAVERY, *courage* (YONG 勇): the ability to face difficult choices; the character quality that deals with the changes of CLIMATE; courage of conviction; willingness to act on vision; one of the six characteristics of a leader.

BREAK, *broken, divided* (PO 破): to DIVIDE what is COMPLETE; the absence of a UNITING PHILOSOPHY; the opposite of UNITY.

CALCULATE, *count,* (SHU 數): mathematical comparison of quantities and qualities; a measurement of DISTANCE or troop size.

CHANGE, *transform* (BIAN 變): transition from one CONDITION to another; the ability to adapt to different situations; a natural characteristic of CLIMATE.

CHAOS, *disorder* (JUAN 亂): CONDITIONS that cannot be FORESEEN; the natural state of confusion arising from BATTLE; one of six weaknesses of an organization; the opposite of CONTROL.

CLAIM, *position, form* (XING 形): to use the GROUND; a shape or specific condition of GROUND; the GROUND that you CONTROL; to use the benefits of the GROUND; the formations of troops; one of the four key skills in making progress.

CLIMATE, *heaven* (TIAN 天): the passage of time; the realm of uncontrollable CHANGE; divine providence; the weather; trends that CHANGE over time; generally, the future; what one must AIM at in the future; one of five key factors in ANALYSIS; the opposite of GROUND.

COMMAND (LING 令): to order or the act of ordering subordinates; the decisions of a LEADER; the creation of METHODS.

COMPETITION: see WAR.

COMPLETE: see UNITY.

CONDITION: see GROUND.

CONFINED, *surround* (WEI 圍): to encircle; a SITUATION or STAGE in which your options are limited; the proper tactic for dealing with an ENEMY that is ten times smaller; to seal off a smaller ENEMY; the characteristic of a STAGE in which a larger FORCE can be attacked by a smaller one; one of nine SITUATIONS or STAGES.

CONFLICT, *fight* (ZHENG 争): to contend; to dispute; direct confrontation of arms with an ENEMY; highly desirable GROUND that creates disputes; one of nine types of GROUND, terrain, or stages.

CONSTRICTED, *narrow* (AI 狹): a confined space or niche; one of six field positions; the limited extreme of the dimension distance; the opposite of SPREAD-OUT.

CONTROL, *govern* (CHI 治): to manage situations; to overcome disorder; the opposite of CHAOS.

DANGEROUS: see SERIOUS.

DANGERS, *adverse,* (AK 阨): a condition that make it difficult to ADVANCE; one of three dimensions used to evaluate advantages; the dimension with the extreme field POSITIONS of ENTANGLING and SUPPORTING.

DEATH, *desperate* (SI 死): to end or the end of life or efforts; an extreme situation in which the only option is BATTLE; one of nine STAGES or types of TERRAIN; one of five types of SPIES; opposite of SURVIVE.

DECEPTION, *bluffing, illusion* (GUI 詭): to control perceptions; to control information; to mislead an ENEMY; an attack on an opponent's AIM; the characteristic of war that confuses perceptions.

DEFEND (SHOU 守): to guard or to hold a GROUND; to remain in a POSITION; the opposite of **ATTACK.**

DETOUR (YU 迂): the indirect or unsuspected path to a POSITION; the more difficult path to ADVANTAGE; the route that is not DIRECT.

DIRECT, *straight* (JIK 直): a straight or obvious path to a goal; opposite of DETOUR.

DISTANCE, *distant* (YUAN 遠): the space separating GROUND; to be remote from the current location; to occupy POSITIONS that are not close to one another; one of six field positions; one of the three dimensions for evaluating opportunities; the emptiness of space.

DIVIDE, *separate* (FEN 分): to break apart a larger force; to separate from a larger group; the opposite of JOIN and FOCUS.

DOUBLE AGENT, *reverse* (FAN 反): to turn around in direction; to change a situation; to switch a person's allegiance; one of five types of spies.

EASY, *light* (QING 輕): to require little effort; a SITUATION that requires little effort; one of nine STAGES or types of terrain; opposite of SERIOUS.

EMOTION, *feeling* (XIN 心): an unthinking reaction to AIM, a necessary element to inspire MOVES; a component of esprit de corps; never a sufficient cause for ATTACK.

ENEMY, *competitor* (DIK 敵): one who desires the same CLAIM; one with a similar GOAL; one with whom comparisons of capabilities are made.

ENTANGLING, *hanging* (GUA 懸): a POSITION that cannot be returned to; any CONDITION that leaves no easy place to go; one of six field positions.

EVADE, *avoid* (BI 避): the tactic used by small competitors when facing large opponents .

FALL APART, *collapse* (BENG 崩): to fail to execute good decisions; to fail to use a CONSTRICTED POSITION; one of six weaknesses of an organization.

FALL DOWN, *sink* (HAAM 陷): to fail to make good decisions; to MOVE from a SUPPORTING POSITION; one of six weaknesses of organizations.

FEELINGS, *affection, love* (CHING 情): the bonds of relationship; the result of a shared PHILOSOPHY; requires management.

FIGHT, *struggle* (DOU 鬥): to engage in CONFLICT; to face difficulties.

FIRE (HUO 火): an environmental weapon; a universal analogy for all weapons.

FLEE, *retreat, northward* (BEI 北): to abandon a POSITION; to surrender GROUND; one of six weaknesses of an ARMY; opposite of ADVANCE.

FOCUS, *concentrate* (ZHUAN 專): to bring resources together at a given time; to UNITE forces for a purpose; an attribute of having a shared PHILOSOPHY; the opposite of *divide*.

FORCE (LEI 力): power in the simplest sense; a GROUP of people bound by UNITY and FOCUS; the relative balance of STRENGTH in opposition to WEAKNESS.

FORESEE: see AIM.

FULLNESS: see STRENGTH.

GENERAL: see LEADER.

GOAL: see PHILOSOPHY.

GROUND, *situation, stage* (DI 地): the earth; a specific place; a specific condition; the place one competes; the prize of competition; one of five key factors in competitive analysis; the opposite of CLIMATE.

GROUPS, *troops* (DUI 隊): a number of people united under a shared PHILOSOPHY; human resources of an organization; one of the five targets of fire attacks.

INSIDE, *internal* (NEI 内): within a TERRITORY or organization; an insider; one of five types of spies; opposite of WAI, outside.

INTERSECTING, *highway* (QU 衢): a SITUATION or GROUND that allows you to JOIN; one of nine types of terrain.

JOIN (HAP 合): to unite; to make allies; to create a larger FORCE; opposite of DIVIDE.

KNOWLEDGE, *listening* (ZHI 知): to have information; the result of listening; the first step in advancing a POSITION; the basis of strategy.

LAX, *loosen* (SHII 弛): too easygoing; lacking discipline; one of six weaknesses of an army.

LEADER, *general, commander* (JIANG 將): the decision-maker in a competitive unit; one who LISTENS and AIMS; one who manages TROOPS; superior of officers and men; one of the five key factors in analysis; the conceptual opposite of FA, the laws, which do not require decisions.

LEARN, *compare* (XIAO 效): to evaluate the relative qualities of ENEMIES.

LISTEN, *obey* (TING 聽): to gather KNOWLEDGE; part of ANALYSIS.

LISTENING: see KNOWLEDGE.

LOCAL, *countryside* (XIANG 鄉): the nearby GROUND; to have KNOWLEDGE of a specific GROUND; one of five types of SPIES.

MARSH (ZE 澤): GROUND where foot-

ing is unstable; one of the four types of GROUND; analogy for uncertain situations.

METHOD: see SYSTEM.

MISSION: see PHILOSOPHY.

MOMENTUM, *influence* (SHI 勢): the FORCE created by SURPRISE set up by STANDARDS; used with TIMING.

MOUNTAINS, *hill, peak* (SHAN 山): uneven GROUND; one of four types of GROUND; an analogy for all unequal SITUATIONS.

MOVE, *march, act* (HANG 行): action toward a position or goal; used as a near synonym for DONG, act.

NATION (GUO 國): the state; the productive part of an organization; the seat of political power; the entity that controls an ARMY or competitive part of the organization.

OBSTACLES, *barricaded* (XIAN 險): to have barriers; one of the three characteristics of the GROUND; one of six field positions; as a field position, opposite of UNOBSTRUCTED.

OPEN, *meeting, crossing* (JIAO 來): to share the same GROUND without conflict; to come together; a SITUATION that encourages a race; one of nine TERRAINS or STAGES.

OPPORTUNITY: see ADVANTAGE.

OUTMANEUVER (SOU 走): to go astray; to be FORCED into a WEAK POSITION; one of six weaknesses of an army.

OUTSIDE, *external* (WAI 外): not within a TERRITORY or ARMY; one who has a different perspective; one who offers an objective view; opposite of INTERNAL.

PHILOSOPHY, *mission, goals* (TAO 道): the shared GOALS that UNITE an ARMY; a system of thought; a shared viewpoint; literally "the way"; a way to work together; one of the five key factors in ANALYSIS.

PLATEAU (LIU 陸): a type of GROUND without defects; an analogy for any equal, solid, and certain SITUATION; the best place for competition; one of the four types of GROUND.

RESOURCES, *provisions* (LIANG 糧): necessary supplies, most commonly food; one of the five targets of fire attacks.

RESTRAINT: see TIMING.

REWARD, *treasure, money* (BAO 賞): profit; wealth; the necessary compensation for competition; a necessary ingredient for VICTORY; VICTORY must pay.

SCATTER, *dissipating* (SAN 散): to disperse; to lose UNITY; the pursuit of separate GOALS as opposed to a central MISSION; a situation that causes a FORCE to scatter; one of nine conditions or types of terrain.

SERIOUS, *heavy* (CHONG 重): any task requiring effort and skill; a SITUATION where resources are running low when you are deeply committed to a campaign or heavily invested in a project; a situation where opposition within an organization mounts; one of nine STAGES or types of TERRAIN.

SIEGE (GONG CHENG 攻城): to move against entrenched positions; any movement against an ENEMY'S STRENGTH; literally "strike city"; one of the four forms of attack; the least desirable form of attack.

SITUATION: see GROUND.

SPEED, *hurry* (SAI 馳): to MOVE over GROUND quickly; the ability to ADVANCE POSITIONS in a minimum of time; needed to take advantage of a window of opportunity.

SPREAD-OUT, *wide* (GUANG 廣): a surplus of DISTANCE; one of the six GROUND POSITIONS; opposite of CONSTRICTED.

SPY, *conduit, go-between* (GAAN 間): a source of information; a channel of communication; literally, an "opening between."

STAGE: see GROUND.

STANDARD, *proper, correct* (JANG 正): the expected behavior; the standard approach; proven methods; the opposite of SURPRISE; together with SURPRISE creates MOMENTUM.

STOREHOUSE, *house* (KU 庫): a place where resources are stockpiled; one of the five targets for fire attacks.

STORES, *accumulate, savings* (JI 糧): resources that have been stored; any type of inventory; one of the five targets of fire attacks.

STRENGTH, *fullness, satisfaction* (SAT 壹): wealth or abundance or resources; the state of being crowded; the opposite of XU, empty.

SUPPLY WAGONS, *transport* (ZI 輜): the movement of RESOURCES through DISTANCE; one of the five targets of fire attacks.

SUPPORT, *supporting* (ZHII 支): to prop up; to enhance; a GROUND POSITION that you cannot leave without losing STRENGTH; one of six field positions; the opposite

extreme of GUA, entangling.

SURPRISE, *unusual, strange* (QI 奇): the unexpected; the innovative; the opposite of STANDARD; together with STANDARDS creates MOMENTUM.

SURROUND: see CONFINED.

SURVIVE, *live, birth* (SHAANG 生): the state of being created, started, or beginning; the state of living or surviving; a temporary condition of fullness; one of five types of spies; the opposite of DEATH.

SYSTEM, *method* (FA 法): a set of procedures; a group of techniques; steps to accomplish a GOAL; one of the five key factors in analysis; the realm of groups who must follow procedures; the opposite of the LEADER.

TERRITORY, *terrain:* see GROUND.

TIMING, *restraint* (JIE 節): to withhold action until the proper time; to release tension; a companion concept to MOMENTUM.

TROOPS: see GROUP.

UNITY, *whole, oneness* (YI 一): the characteristic of a GROUP that shares a PHILOSOPHY; the lowest number; a GROUP that acts as a unit; the opposite DIVIDED.

UNOBSTRUCTED, *expert* (TONG 通): without obstacles or barriers; GROUND that allows easy movement; open to new ideas; one of six field positions; opposite of OBSTRUCTED.

VICTORY, *win, winning* (SING 勝): success in an endeavor; getting a reward; serving your mission; an event that produces more than it consumes; to make a profit.

WAR, *competition, army* (BING 兵): a dynamic situation in which POSITIONS can be won or lost; a contest in which a REWARD can be won; the conditions under which the rules of strategy work.

WATER, *river* (SHUI 水): a fast-changing GROUND; fluid CONDITIONS; one of four types of GROUND; an analogy for change.

WEAKNESS, *emptiness, need* (XU 處): the absence of people or resources; devoid of FORCE; the point of ATTACK for an ADVANTAGE; a characteristic of GROUND that enables SPEED; poor; the opposite of STRENGTh.

WIN, *winning:* see VICTORY.

WIND, *fashion, custom* (FENG 風): the pressure of environmental forces.

Index of Topics in *The Art of War*

This index identifies significant topics, keyed to the chapters, block numbers (big numbers in text), and line numbers (tiny numbers). The format is chapter:block.lines.

Join the Science of Strategy Institute
www.ScienceOfStrategy.com

Become the complete strategist!

Book Programs
Library Memberships
Book Club Memberships
Books and Audios

On-Line Training Programs
The Warrior Class
The Strategy School

Academy of Strategy
On-Line Strategic Training
The Academy Library
Personalized Advice on Strategy

Institute Seminars and Training
A Worldwide Network of Trainers
Internal Corporate Licensing

About the Author

Gary Gagliardi, the founder of the Science of Strategy Institute and the award-winning author of over a dozen books on strategy, started in business as a successful entrepreneur. To learn more about his books and seminar programs, visit **www.scienceofstrategy.com**.